# Start Investing with Robo-Advisors

# Start Investing with Robo-Advisors

## Let smart algorithms grow your portfolio while you live your life

Elias Hartwell

Mindful Pages

Published in 2025

ISBN: 9789371771801 (PB)
ISBN: 9789371777995 (eBook)

*Published by*

**Mindful Pages**
*Imprint of Alpha Editions LLC*
312 W. 2nd St #1834
Casper, WY 82601, USA


This book was developed using advanced writing tools to support the drafting and ideation process. All content has been thoughtfully curated, refined, and reviewed to ensure quality and relevance.

# Content

# Introduction
# The Wisdom of Letting Go

There is a quiet rebellion stirring in the realm of personal finance—one that makes no spectacle of itself. No shouting pundits, no scrolling tickers demanding attention. Its signature is silence. It is the hush of people stepping away, of choosing not to hover over every market tremor, not to watch the screen with tightened fists and darting eyes. These are not the disinterested or the careless. Far from it. They are intentional, awake to the bigger picture, and startlingly pragmatic. They have stumbled upon an idea so plain it feels almost heretical: the wisest move, sometimes, is to loosen your grip.

This book is for them. And for those prepared to follow.

For much of modern memory, the language of money has been martial. Finance was framed as combat, with investors as soldiers—perpetually alert, endlessly calculating, ready to strike. Wealth was depicted as spoils of war, handed to those who stared longest at the charts, who pursued every flicker of opportunity, who equated exhaustion with control. Mastery was the idol: learn enough, care enough, monitor closely enough, and you might bend the market to your will.

But over decades, evidence has told another story. The harder we try to outsmart the market, the further behind we fall. Effort mutates into inefficiency. Tinkering piles up costs—fees, wasted time, frayed nerves. Obsession corrodes our connection to money itself, transforming sensible engagement into compulsive interference, the human attempt to outmuscle uncertainty. What begins as prudence too often curdles into pathology.

It is not merely unproductive. It is dehumanising.

Into this weary landscape step robo-advisors. At first glance, their presence seems incongruous. Cold algorithms, impersonal dashboards, portfolios spun from code. Their branding leans sterile, their design suspiciously frictionless. Yet look past the polish and something more intriguing appears: an invitation to treat money differently. Not as a wild beast needing constant handling, but as a system deserving of structure and trust.

This book regards robo-advisors not as shortcuts for the naive, nor as shiny gadgets for the disengaged, but as vehicles of liberation. They free us—not from responsibility, but from its distortions. They do not replace wisdom; they redirect it. They allow us to step away from frantic micromanagement and stand instead as architects, shaping a financial foundation sturdy enough to support the lives we want to live.

But such a step takes courage. Not the thrill-seeking bravado of the day trader, but the quieter, harder courage of restraint. The courage to allow, to delegate, to trust. To release the illusion of control and find in its place a steadier kind of agency.

Because letting go is not the same as giving up. It is choosing a higher order of freedom.

To be clear, this is no catalogue of robo-advisors ranked by their fees or app design. We will touch on these, but they are not the heart of the matter. The essence of this book lies elsewhere: in the psychology of why we invest as we do, why we cling to myths of prediction and mastery, why we confuse motion with progress, and why, in a world drowning in alerts and analysis, true wisdom may lie in the audacity of simplification.

Letting go, then, is not simply financial. It is philosophical.

We inhabit a culture that fetishises busyness, that exalts the hustle as a virtue. To pause is to waste. This restlessness seeps into how we handle wealth. We are trained to monitor, adjust, optimise without pause. To chase returns, fight downturns, seize fleeting spikes. And when we do not, we are made to feel negligent.

But what if this premise itself is flawed? What if the advantage does not belong to the busiest investor but the most consistent one? What if the true edge lies not in sharper knowledge, but in steadier behaviour?

Here lies the deeper argument for robo-advisors. They are not gadgets of convenience; they are guardrails for the mind. They shield us from ourselves, steadying our impulses, filtering noise into discipline. They dissolve the fantasy that we must "know everything" before acting, granting us instead the space to live while our portfolios quietly work.

That freedom is no trivial gain.

Consider the endless energy wasted in monitoring portfolios, the sleepless hum of "Am I doing enough?" The compulsive tapping of apps, the obsessive news alerts. Think of the mental clutter. Now imagine reclaiming that bandwidth. Imagine investments compounding in rhythm with your values while you pour your focus into relationships, pursuits, and projects that imbue life with its actual worth.

This book is a manual for that reclamation.

We begin with the beliefs that govern us—unseen, inherited, and stubborn. How our families, cultures, and fears hardwire us to equate control with safety. How this equation tempts us into exhausting, futile strategies. We will unmask the modern addiction to financial "noise"—the streams of commentary that simulate knowledge even as they muddy perspective.

From there, we will examine robo-advisors themselves—not just their mechanics, but their meaning. The principles embedded in their algorithms. The economic truths they formalise. The psychological myths they quietly dismantle. What it signifies, emotionally, to delegate. What it demands of us, philosophically, to trust a system crafted to be more patient, more consistent, than we are capable of being alone.

We will then argue, with the support of behavioural science, for intelligent surrender. Not abdication, but alignment. Not shrinking from responsibility, but reshaping it. At times, the wisest move is not to place yourself at the centre of every fluctuation, but to step back and allow systems stronger than your impulses to carry the weight.

Practicalities follow. How to select a platform that reflects your values. How to discern your true appetite for risk—the one revealed under stress, not in abstract thought. How to design goals that resonate both mathematically and emotionally. How to erect a structure in mere hours that could sustain you for decades.

We will explore how automation serves as ballast against turbulent markets. How rebalancing, tax-loss harvesting, automatic deposits—so often dismissed as "features"—are in fact the bones of a coherent philosophy. We will outline how to ritualise financial check-ins, so engagement becomes meaningful habit rather than anxious reflex.

And then, the shadows: the traps of overconfidence, the myth of instinct, the folklore investors spin from isolated triumphs or losses. We will probe the emotional cost of DIY obsession and offer alternatives rooted in reason, not ego.

Finally, we expand outward. No single model works the same everywhere. Tax codes shift across borders, cultural expectations alter behaviours, access varies. We will survey these differences, offering ways to adapt while remaining grounded in the central ethic of simplicity. And as life itself changes—with marriage, children, career upheavals, or age—we will consider how to let your system bend with you, not against you.

This book is not a call to chase alpha. It is a call to craft alignment. To design a financial structure that enriches not only your account but your attention. A structure that yields both returns and release.

In the chapters ahead, we will unsettle certain orthodoxies. We will trade vigilance for clarity, micromanagement for meaning. And we will argue that the wisest investors of tomorrow may not be those who strain hardest, but those who have learned the rare skill of stepping back.

So breathe. Step off the treadmill. The aim here is not victory in some imagined contest. It is the creation of a life.

Let us begin.

# Chapter 1
# Why We Obsess Over Money—and What It Costs Us

Money today is far more than a medium of exchange. It has swollen into a mirror, a ruler, a report card, and—too often—a quiet tyrant. It tells us how we measure up, steers our decisions, and steals our attention. Yet beneath the surface of budgets, spreadsheets, and targets lies something murkier: an inherited belief system about money, usually unexamined, that operates in the background of our lives. We convince ourselves our choices are rational, guided by calculation. In truth, many of them are performances—echoes of cultural scripts, half-remembered family lessons, or attempts to hush anxieties that numbers alone cannot soothe.

The starting point is uncomfortable but necessary: most people are not investing to grow wealth; they are investing to feel safe. Or to feel competent, accomplished, in control. These motives are understandable, human even, but they cloud the ability to make decisions that endure. Left unchecked, they provoke habits that look strategic but are really emotional reactions—restless trading, compulsive portfolio checks, hurried sales during downturns, needless over-diversification, or a chase after whatever fad is dressed up as "opportunity." Behind each act lies a psyche seeking reassurance, trying to fix an inner unease with financial instruments.

This conditioning begins early. For many, money first appears not as an abstract idea but as tension—rows between parents, whispered fears about bills, or envy of those who had more. Scarcity, or its opposite, abundance, plants seeds that harden into beliefs. These scripts calcify into an operating system beneath our awareness. They influence our appetite for risk, our sense of what we deserve, our definition of success. Some learn to treat thrift as a moral virtue. Others stitch money to identity: the provider, the entrepreneur, the shrewd investor. And many internalise the notion that security is nothing more than the number blinking in the bank account.

Such beliefs rarely announce themselves plainly. They surface as whispers. Anxiety at the sight of a red line on a graph. Doubt after reading a headline. The subtle thrill of information mistaken for control. They reward hyper-engagement and cast stillness as negligence. Worst of all, they promote the fantasy that markets can be conquered, not simply understood.

The architecture of modern investing worsens the trap. Platforms are not austere tools for long-term planning; they are laboratories of stimulation. Bright dashboards, pulsing charts, constant feeds, and alerts engineered to pull the mind back again and again. Less library, more casino—designed for immersion, not reflection. Checking has replaced choosing. Portfolios are refreshed, tracked, even scrolled, as if they were social media feeds or sports scores. What feels like empowerment is, in many cases, little more than access dressed up as wisdom.

The issue is not the access itself but the way we respond to it. We mistake quantity of data for quality of insight. We imagine attention equals diligence, that staring at markets equals responsibility. But misplaced attention corrodes conviction. It shortens horizons. It fuels reaction over reason.

This compulsive involvement is often defended as discipline. Yet more often it is fear in disguise. Fear of missing out, of lagging behind, of being caught unprepared. And so, in the pursuit of freedom, we chain ourselves to volatility. We tell ourselves we are prudent when we are, in fact, trapped in cycles of overthinking and overmanagement. It is not strategy at all—it is compensation for unease.

Take Rahul, a gifted software engineer who plunged into equities after a promotion. He consumed trading guides, charting tools, timing strategies. He was sincere in his belief: study hard, act fast, and he could outperform. Early wins came, but so did restless nights. His phone never left his hand. Weekends dissolved into research. Every dip felt like a judgment on his intelligence. Within a year, his portfolio was stagnant, but his stress had doubled. Switching to a passive, automated portfolio was not a financial calculation, he later admitted, but a psychological release.

Rahul's path is hardly unusual. It is not a failure of intellect but a symptom of a culture that ties competence to control. To step back feels like weakness; to watch calmly feels negligent. Yet the cost is steep—not just in returns but in time, clarity, peace of mind.

Time especially is undervalued. We chase incremental gains without tallying the hours drained in pursuit. The financial world convinces us every fraction of a percent is victory, while the time we spend clawing for it goes uncounted. This is the hidden crisis of investing today: poverty of time. We make spreadsheets for money but not for attention. We pile up assets yet run deficits in presence.

This chapter presses on that imbalance. It asks: what are you really purchasing when you over-manage? Safety? Status? A fragile sense of control? And what is the price?

To answer, we must uncover the hidden scaffolding of financial thought. We will challenge the myths that bind money to virtue, intelligence, or worth. We will expose how platforms are designed not just to inform but to ensnare. And we will trace how fear, camouflaged as diligence, manipulates our behaviour.

We will also look at noise. Not merely the clamour of media, but the inner static—the "should haves" and "what ifs" that pile up with every chart refresh. You will see how excess input distorts judgement, and why, paradoxically, knowing less can sometimes mean acting better. Knowledge itself is not the enemy; the lack of discernment is.

And then, we will begin to reframe. Wealth not as stockpiles, but as coherence: alignment between financial choices and the shape of your actual life. Central to that reframing is time—how you spend it, how you honour it. For the greatest return of letting go is not efficiency alone, but the restoration of focus. The ability to direct your gaze away from flashing numbers and towards the parts of life that matter.

To let go is not to be careless. It is to care wisely, to build a system and trust it. It is to know that true financial intelligence lies not in omniscience, but in discernment—choosing what not to chase. It is to remember that money should not command your attention, but release it.

This chapter is an invitation. To step back, not out. To exchange obsession for clarity, compulsion for rhythm. To recognise that by relinquishing the need to control every tick of the market, you reclaim something infinitely more precious: your time, your focus, your freedom.

## The Hidden Beliefs We Don't Know We're Carrying

Ask most people why they invest, and their answers will appear rational: to build wealth, to secure retirement, to outpace inflation, to ensure their children's future. These are textbook responses—economically sound, logically coherent, and broadly accepted. But dig beneath the surface, and a more complex truth emerges: many of our financial decisions are less about strategy than about identity. Our investing behaviours are not shaped in sterile vacuums of reason, but in the messy environments of childhood memory, cultural inheritance, social comparison, and deeply held—often unconscious—beliefs about what money represents.

Money is never just money. It is a proxy for control, competence, safety, status, or even self-worth. And when we operate without examining the symbolic meanings we attach to it, we risk confusing emotional needs with financial goals. The consequence is not only poor investment choices, but a distorted relationship with wealth itself—one characterised by restlessness, guilt, anxiety, or compulsive effort. We are not merely trying to grow capital. We are, in many cases, trying to resolve something far more personal.

Consider how culture encodes these meanings. In much of Western society, money is framed as a moral indicator—those who have it are perceived as more disciplined, intelligent, or hard-working. Success stories are financial stories; the "self-made millionaire" is held up as a secular saint. From this perspective, wealth is not just a resource but a measure of merit. The investor becomes a kind of moral actor, and losses are not just unfortunate—they are interpreted as personal failings. This moralisation of money leads to a kind of perfectionism around finances: constant monitoring, compulsive optimisation, and an aversion to delegation that borders on superstition. After all, if wealth proves worth, outsourcing investment decisions feels like outsourcing one's identity.

In contrast, many Asian cultures, particularly those shaped by Confucian or collectivist values, frame money as duty. Financial success is not just personal—it's familial. The accumulation and preservation of wealth is a form of honouring one's parents and securing the wellbeing of future generations. Here, money becomes not a mark of merit but of responsibility. Risk tolerance is tempered by the weight of intergenerational obligation. The idea of "losing" money carries not just economic but emotional cost, as it is tied to failure in fulfilling one's expected role in the family system.

Then there are post-colonial and post-conflict societies, where wealth may carry undertones of survival and power. Money represents protection—against instability, government failure, or the memory of scarcity. Here, cash in hand, gold under the mattress, or property in a safe jurisdiction may feel more "real" than any long-term portfolio. Investing becomes less about future orientation and more about immediate security—sometimes at the expense of long-term optimisation.

These cultural lenses do not stay abstract. They shape the actual portfolios people construct. They influence whether one seeks growth or security, whether one believes in the wisdom of the market or suspects it's a rigged game, whether one views delegation as intelligent or irresponsible. And because these lenses are internalised so early and reinforced so subtly, we often cannot see them operating. They become the default backdrop against which all financial decisions are made.

Inherited family narratives deepen this effect. Many of us are living out economic scripts written by generations before us. A parent who grew up during a recession might instil a deep fear of loss, leading their children to become excessively conservative, even when conditions have changed. A family culture that equates wealth with virtue may produce adults who chase performance not for practical needs, but to prove moral adequacy. These beliefs are not formally taught. They are modelled in language, tone, and behaviour—what is praised, what is condemned, what is considered "smart" or "foolish."

The tragedy is that most investors are unaware of these scripts. They attribute their decisions to analysis, when in fact they are acting from emotion masked as logic. A professional who refuses to delegate their portfolio management may claim it's about staying informed—but in reality, they might associate control with competence, and fear that letting go implies inadequacy. Another might compulsively diversify across dozens of asset classes—not because it's optimal, but because childhood experiences of volatility taught them that safety lies in spreading risk thinly, even irrationally.

Fear often disguises itself as strategy. A common example is overtrading. On the surface, it seems like engagement—keeping on top of market moves, responding to opportunities. But often, it is a response to discomfort. Doing something, anything, feels safer than doing nothing. The investor is not reacting to the market; they are reacting to their anxiety. Similarly, an obsession with financial news may be justified as staying "well-informed," but beneath that habit may lie a deep fear of being blindsided, of missing out, or of being judged as careless. The behaviour is logical on its surface, but emotionally compulsive underneath.

This is not a call to pathologise every financial decision. Nor is it an argument for disengagement. Rather, it is a reminder that investing is never purely about numbers. It is an emotionally charged, psychologically complex activity that exposes our deepest beliefs about risk, security, status, and self. Recognising this is not weakness—it is maturity. It allows us to approach the market with clearer eyes, and to design systems that serve our actual values rather than our unconscious fears.

Modern investing culture makes this reflection harder, not easier. The rise of algorithmic trading, gamified investing apps, and endless market commentary accelerates decision-making but discourages introspection. We are pushed to act, not to understand. The result is a strange irony: we have more access to financial tools than ever before, and yet our financial thinking is increasingly shallow. We trade fast but reflect slowly. We optimise returns while ignoring the psychological frameworks that shape those returns. We automate everything—except our self-awareness.

To move beyond this, we need a more honest conversation about what money represents to us personally. Not just as investors, but as individuals shaped by time, place, family, and culture. What did your upbringing teach you about having—or not having—money? What emotions surface when you think about risk? How do you feel when you let go of control? These questions are not esoteric. They are foundational. Until we examine the beliefs we carry, we cannot consciously choose whether to keep or discard them.

There is also an ethical dimension to this awareness. When we operate from unexamined beliefs, we tend to impose them on others—partners, children, employees. We mistake our story for the story. A parent with a high-risk tolerance may pressure their child into aggressive investment choices, projecting confidence as wisdom. A financially anxious spouse may veto long-term strategies in favour of immediate liquidity, framing caution as prudence. These dynamics are rarely about right or wrong—they are about misalignment. And misalignment, over time, corrodes trust and clarity.

Clarity, then, becomes the real asset. Not market foresight or algorithmic precision, but a conscious understanding of the architecture beneath your decisions. Clarity allows you to delegate wisely, rather than resist out of fear. It helps you set goals that reflect your values, not inherited scripts. It enables you to step back—not as an abdication, but as an act of intelligence.

Robo-advisors, at their best, offer more than automation. They offer a mirror. By asking you to articulate your risk tolerance, your goals, your time horizon, they force a degree of self-reflection that traditional investing often bypasses. They remove the illusion that you are in control of markets, and redirect your attention to the one thing you *can* control: the quality of your decisions, and the clarity of your motivations.

But this clarity is only possible if you are willing to confront the stories you've been telling yourself about money. Not to discard them all, but to examine them honestly. Are they still serving you? Or are they keeping you in patterns that no longer match your life?

This is the hidden work of investing—the inner portfolio, so to speak. It is less visible, less quantifiable, but no less powerful. Because until we understand *why* we invest the way we do, we cannot fully align our strategies with our values. And without alignment, even the most optimised portfolio becomes a hollow exercise—financially active, but psychologically inert.

To carry unexamined beliefs about money is not a personal failing. It is the default condition of modern life. But to illuminate those beliefs—to ask where they came from, whether they still belong, and how they affect our choices—is the beginning of true financial intelligence. Not just intelligence measured in returns, but in peace, clarity, and purpose. And that, ultimately, is what wealth is for.

## Fear Disguised as Strategy

One of the most quietly destructive forces in modern investing is fear masquerading as intelligence. It is not the overt panic that tanks markets during crashes or fuels selling frenzies—it is subtler, more socially acceptable, and far more persistent. It presents itself as vigilance, as rational scepticism, as "staying informed." It often comes wrapped in the language of prudence and precision. But underneath it all, it is anxiety in disguise. And that anxiety is not only exhausting—it's expensive.

Active investing has long been marketed as the path of the serious investor. To trade frequently, to tweak and rebalance often, to chase earnings reports and act on forecasts—these behaviours are lauded as signs of commitment and financial literacy. They offer the illusion of control in a world characterised by uncertainty. But as research consistently shows, active management is less correlated with superior returns than with superior stress. The more often we intervene, the more we expose ourselves to poor timing, behavioural biases, and unnecessary fees. Over time, the data is unambiguous: most active investors underperform both the market and their own intentions.

The question is: if active investing is so often counterproductive, why do so many intelligent people persist in doing it?

The answer lies not in knowledge, but in emotion. Specifically, fear—fear of missing out, fear of being caught unprepared, fear of appearing incompetent, fear of regret. These fears rarely announce themselves. They are rationalised through elaborate explanations, market narratives, or economic commentary. Investors believe they are acting on insight, when they are often reacting to discomfort. This dynamic is not just common—it is foundational to much of what drives modern financial behaviour.

Consider the case of Linda, a 42-year-old professional working in corporate law in London. With a strong academic background and a diligent personality, she approached her finances with the same rigour she brought to her career. She subscribed to multiple financial newsletters, read earnings reports over breakfast, and monitored her portfolio daily. She believed this level of involvement was a mark of responsibility. Yet after five years, her performance lagged behind a basic index fund, despite countless hours of analysis. She wasn't irrational—her trades were justified by technical indicators and market commentary. But what she didn't see was the emotional pattern beneath her activity. Every significant market movement triggered a sense of unease. Doing nothing felt negligent. Action, even if unprofitable, gave her psychological relief. Her portfolio was her proxy for control in a world that offered little certainty.

This story is not unique. It is the default mode for many highly capable individuals—those who are disciplined in their professions but carry unexamined anxiety into their investments. The financial world encourages this by equating movement with mastery. Brokerage platforms are designed to incentivise trading. Financial media rarely rewards stillness. Every headline screams for attention; every analysis ends with a call to action. The cumulative effect is an environment in which inaction feels like failure, and silence feels irresponsible.

This illusion of control is seductive. It satisfies the deep human need to do something in the face of uncertainty. The markets are complex, opaque, and often irrational. Our impulse is to intervene, to act, to manage the chaos. But most of what feels like control is noise management. We are not improving outcomes—we are managing emotions. And often, those emotions are rooted in fear.

The cognitive science behind this is well-documented. Behavioural finance identifies a host of biases—loss aversion, overconfidence, recency bias, confirmation bias—that compromise our judgement. But beneath these biases is a simpler truth: the human brain is poorly wired for long-term investing. We are evolutionarily primed to respond to threat, to seek immediate feedback, to act on perceived patterns. The stock market exploits all of these tendencies. Its volatility mirrors threat. Its daily movements offer a never-ending stream of feedback. And its randomness can be easily mistaken for meaningful patterns. The result is a psychological minefield in which rational strategy is constantly undermined by emotional impulse.

This is where the façade of strategy becomes most dangerous. Investors often don't recognise that their behaviour is driven by discomfort. The language of analysis provides cover. "I reallocated because of macroeconomic indicators." "I sold tech because of Q2 earnings volatility." "I'm staying liquid in case of a correction." Each statement may be grounded in some reality—but that does not make it the product of rational planning. Fear, once dressed in financial jargon, becomes difficult to distinguish from prudence.

The impact is not just psychological. It is cumulative and compounding. Every unnecessary trade incurs costs—both explicit (fees, taxes, spreads) and implicit (mistimed exits, missed recoveries). But beyond performance, there is also the hidden cost of cognitive load. Constant vigilance depletes attention. It increases anxiety. It reduces bandwidth for other areas of life. One could argue that the most under-discussed cost of active investing is not underperformance, but burnout.

Take the example of Marcus, a software entrepreneur in Bangalore, who began investing aggressively after selling his first company. He immersed himself in financial education, followed markets across time zones, and began managing a portfolio of 40 individual stocks, supplemented by options positions and alternative assets. On paper, he was diversifying. In reality, he was overwhelmed. Each day brought a new set of decisions. Every global news event felt urgent. After two years, his returns were marginally positive—but his mental health had deteriorated. He described feeling "trapped in a second job I never wanted." What he initially framed as strategic involvement had, in practice, become a full-time performance anxiety loop.

This is the point at which many investors begin to reassess. Not because they've failed, but because they've realised the real cost of always being "on." The recognition that action is not always agency—and that in financial matters, restraint is often the highest form of discipline—is a turning point in an investor's maturity.

Yet even then, letting go is difficult. Not because the evidence isn't persuasive, but because the identity of the active investor is hard to relinquish. For many, being involved equals being smart, being responsible, being capable. Surrendering control can feel like surrendering competence. It requires a reframing—not of strategy, but of self-concept. One must learn to see delegation not as disengagement, but as design. As a decision to prioritise clarity over activity, outcomes over effort, and peace of mind over constant motion.

This is where robo-advisors offer a subtle but powerful intervention. Their value is not only in optimisation or automation. It is in interruption. They interrupt the cycle of emotional over-involvement by imposing constraints. They offer structured allocation, disciplined rebalancing, and long-term orientation—not because these are the only paths to returns, but because they reduce the opportunity for fear-driven meddling. By design, they make it harder to act impulsively. They allow the investor to *design* a strategy, and then *trust* it—rather than feel compelled to tweak it endlessly.

This shift—away from performance theatre and toward structural trust—is not just behavioural. It is philosophical. It requires a recognition that uncertainty is not a problem to be solved, but a condition to be lived with. It demands that we see investing not as a test of our intellect, but as a practice in emotional regulation. And it asks a deeper question: what are we really trying to achieve when we say we want control?

Because control, in most cases, is not about markets. It is about self. The desire to act, to optimise, to stay ahead—these are not inherently financial urges. They are expressions of deeper psychological patterns. Until we recognise that, we remain vulnerable to a kind of strategic self-deception—acting from fear, while calling it foresight.

True financial intelligence lies in the capacity to distinguish between signal and noise, between action and reaction, between strategy and self-soothing. This requires more than technical knowledge. It demands emotional literacy. It requires us to ask, not only "What is the market doing?" but "What is driving me to respond?" That second question is harder—but far more important.

Letting go of unnecessary control is not about passive investing. It is about conscious investing. It is the discipline of designing a plan that reflects your values, your goals, and your temperament—and then having the courage to follow it. Not blindly, but calmly. Not reactively, but deliberately.

Because the opposite of fear is not recklessness. It is clarity. And clarity, in investing as in life, is rarely found in the frantic pursuit of control. It is found in the steady discipline of letting the system do its work, while you focus on yours.

## Noise Addiction in the Financial Age

There was a time when investors received news from the morning paper, consulted a trusted adviser, and reviewed their portfolios on a quarterly basis—perhaps less. Today, the average investor checks their portfolio multiple times a day, consumes news in real time, and is bombarded by alerts, commentary, and analysis from a saturated digital environment. The sheer velocity of financial information has shifted from a tool of insight to a source of compulsion. And yet, paradoxically, as information has become more abundant, clarity has become more elusive.

The modern investor does not suffer from a lack of access, but from an excess of stimulus.

This overstimulation is not accidental. Financial media outlets compete for attention in a crowded landscape. Brokerage apps are designed with the psychology of habit formation in mind. Chart updates, earnings announcements, trend notifications, and volatility alerts are crafted not merely to inform—but to provoke. The result is a steady drip of dopamine that mirrors the reward cycles found in social media, gaming, and gambling platforms. Every update delivers a hit of urgency. Every market swing is framed as actionable. Every news item arrives wrapped in implied consequence.

What's at stake here is not just productivity, but perception. The investor begins to mistake movement for meaning, activity for control, and consumption for strategy. This is the illusion of empowerment: the sense that by staying informed, one is acting wisely. But insight is not the same as awareness, and attention does not guarantee discernment. As the volume of input increases, our ability to distinguish signal from noise degrades. We may feel more engaged, but we are not necessarily more effective.

Consider the cognitive mechanics at work. The human brain evolved to react to immediate threats, not to process abstract, probabilistic data. We are biologically hardwired for short-termism. Recency bias leads us to overweight the latest information. Availability bias means we give undue weight to the most vivid or emotionally charged headlines. The more frequent the data stream, the more we are pulled into reactivity. And reactivity is the enemy of rational investing.

This distortion plays out visibly in behaviour. Retail investors who track the market daily are significantly more likely to trade impulsively, react to short-term volatility, and deviate from long-term plans. The 24-hour market news cycle, amplified by app alerts and trending tickers, encourages micro-assessments of performance—what was gained or lost today, this hour, even this minute. But good investing happens on a different timescale. Long-term returns are not built in daily intervals. They require patience, discipline, and the ability to endure discomfort without overreacting. The investor who cannot tune out the noise is effectively robbed of these essential traits.

The psychology of habit formation reinforces this trap. Every time an investor opens a market app and sees a green arrow, there is a mild sense of reward. A red arrow triggers a jolt of anxiety. This reward-punishment cycle builds addictive engagement. Apps like Robinhood, which pioneered the gamification of trading, are only the most obvious examples. But even reputable platforms use behavioural design to keep users engaged. Interface design, notification frequency, and language choice all conspire to keep the investor looking, checking, reacting. This is not education—it's reinforcement.

The problem is compounded by the cultural valorisation of staying informed. In professional environments, attentiveness is praised. In financial circles, ignorance is stigmatised. The investor who disengages is seen as naïve or negligent. But this overlooks a vital distinction: *selective ignorance is not the same as irresponsibility*. In fact, the ability to deliberately filter out irrelevant information is a hallmark of strategic thinking. The wise investor does not consume everything—they consume carefully. They understand that *not all knowledge is worth having in real time*.

This selective attention is precisely what financial noise undermines. When every piece of news is framed as urgent, none of it feels optional. The emotional bandwidth required to triage information becomes overwhelming. Decision fatigue sets in. The investor, unsure of what matters, starts to act from a place of anxiety rather than conviction. Over time, this erodes both performance and confidence.

Consider a study conducted by Barber and Odean, which found that individual investors who traded more frequently underperformed those who traded less. Their research showed that most active trades were prompted by news flow or market volatility—inputs that appeared informative but, in fact, drove poor timing. The more investors engaged with financial media, the more likely they were to make changes that hurt rather than helped. It wasn't ignorance that cost them; it was hyper-engagement.

Real-world examples illustrate this with painful clarity. During the COVID-19 market crash in March 2020, millions of retail investors liquidated portfolios in response to plunging indices and panic-stricken headlines. The media ecosystem was saturated with dire predictions—some of them warranted, many of them speculative. Those who acted on these signals often missed the swift rebound that followed, locking in losses and delaying recovery. Meanwhile, those who were less exposed to the noise—those who delegated, automated, or simply disengaged—were statistically more likely to have stayed invested and benefited from the recovery.

This is not an argument against financial literacy. It is a call for financial sanity. The goal is not to become ignorant of the world, but to develop a disciplined relationship with information. To know when to listen, and when to mute. To know which inputs enhance understanding, and which simply agitate. The investor must move from passive consumer to active curator.

But doing so requires confronting a deeper psychological truth: *we crave noise because it gives us the illusion of agency*. When the market is unpredictable, watching it feels like doing something. Refreshing an app every hour feels like vigilance. Subscribing to newsletters, checking Twitter, scanning analyst predictions—these are behaviours that satisfy our need to "stay on top of things." But they are often rituals of control, not strategies of effectiveness.

This insight has implications for how we structure our investing environment. Just as we know that willpower alone is insufficient to change eating habits, we must recognise that resisting noise requires more than self-discipline—it requires system design. This is one of the great advantages of using robo-advisors or automated investment platforms. They create a barrier between impulse and action. By automating rebalancing, contributions, and asset allocation, they eliminate the need to constantly decide. More importantly, they shield the investor from the daily noise that so often leads to costly overreaction.

Automation, in this context, is not just about efficiency—it is about insulation. It protects the investor from themselves, not by suppressing intelligence, but by filtering the inputs that degrade it. The irony is striking: the less information one engages with, the more stable their investing behaviour tends to be. Clarity is found not in accumulating more input, but in removing distraction.

This also reframes the meaning of financial sophistication. The skilled investor is not the one who knows the most in real time. It is the one who knows how to identify what is *worth knowing*, and when. It is the one who understands that *timing the market* is less important than *spending time in the market*. It is the one who resists the compulsion to act on every stimulus and instead focuses on the structural, behavioural, and philosophical foundations of sound investing.

To break the addiction to financial noise is not to become passive. It is to become intentional. It is to reject the illusion that more input always leads to better outcomes. It is to acknowledge that the brain, brilliant as it is, has limitations—and that building guardrails is not a concession, but a form of mastery.

Ultimately, the task of the modern investor is not to chase more data, but to reclaim attention. To step outside the volatility theatre and ask: what actually deserves my focus? What serves my long-term vision, and what merely feeds my short-term emotion?

Because the price of constant engagement is not just bad decisions—it is lost clarity. And clarity, unlike information, cannot be downloaded. It must be cultivated. Deliberately. Quietly. And without noise.

## The Quiet Crisis: Time Poverty in the Age of Optimisation

If wealth were measured not in currency but in attention, many affluent individuals would be shockingly poor. Their calendars are full, their portfolios are managed down to the decimal point, their news feeds are refreshed hourly. Yet beneath the outward success is a subtle erosion: of focus, of presence, of peace. It is not financial insecurity that afflicts them, but *time poverty*—a condition in which every spare moment becomes collateral damage in the relentless pursuit of efficiency and control. We speak of optimising wealth, but rarely ask: *at what cost?*

This subchapter is not about financial illiteracy or economic hardship. It is about an intelligent, ambitious class of investors who, in their determination to manage every financial variable, gradually lose track of the one resource they cannot reclaim: time. They believe they are buying freedom, but they are spending attention. They think they are building autonomy, but they are surrendering clarity. The modern cult of financial optimisation—micromanagement, constant rebalancing, compulsive research—promises control but often delivers distraction.

To understand this phenomenon, we must first reframe the concept of wealth. For centuries, wealth has been synonymous with accumulation: of assets, income streams, and influence. But accumulation is only half the story. *Real wealth is the ability to direct your attention toward what you value most.* It is the autonomy to decide not just how you earn, but how you live. When time becomes secondary to money—even in the name of financial security—we are no longer wealth builders. We are wealth custodians trapped in an endless task list, managing a life we barely have time to live.

Consider Rajiv, a 39-year-old executive at a multinational firm in Singapore. By all traditional metrics, Rajiv is thriving: he earns a seven-figure salary, owns property in multiple countries, and has invested in over twenty different financial products ranging from index funds to structured notes. But in conversation, a different picture emerges. Rajiv spends his evenings reading market updates, his weekends running simulations in Excel, and his holidays glued to his investment apps. He claims to enjoy the process, but admits to waking at 3 a.m. to check for geopolitical updates that might affect his emerging markets allocation. His portfolio has become not a source of freedom, but a full-time mental occupation.

Rajiv's story is increasingly common. Technology has made it easier than ever to access financial markets. But with that access comes an expectation—spoken or unspoken—that we must always be managing, tweaking, adjusting. The culture of personal finance subtly valorises the investor who "stays on top of it." Passive investing, though statistically proven to outperform in many cases, is still regarded by many as insufficiently vigilant. In this landscape, *stillness is mistaken for irresponsibility*, and peace of mind for complacency.

This mindset is reinforced by the prevailing language of optimisation. Investors are told to maximise returns, minimise fees, rebalance frequently, tax-harvest strategically, and monitor macroeconomic indicators. Each of these tasks, in isolation, may be sound. But collectively, they create an operating system in which financial life becomes *yet another arena of perfectionism*. And like all perfectionism, it steals joy under the guise of diligence.

We must ask what is being optimised and for whom. If a 0.4% gain in annual returns requires 200 hours of analysis and constant psychological tension, is that truly optimisation? The arithmetic of investing does not account for emotional labour. No performance chart shows the cost of missed conversations, distracted weekends, or minds that can't switch off. *Yet these are real, measurable losses*—they just don't appear on the spreadsheet.

This phenomenon becomes clearer when viewed through the lens of cognitive load. Human attention is finite. Every task we perform, every decision we make, every app we check consumes mental energy. Research in behavioural science shows that decision fatigue reduces the quality of our choices, particularly in high-stakes domains like finance. The more decisions we force ourselves to make—regardless of their importance—the less clarity we bring to any of them. Constant micromanagement of investments may feel productive, but it diminishes our overall cognitive and emotional resilience.

There is also a deeper philosophical dimension to time poverty: its impact on meaning. Time is not just a resource—it is the canvas on which we create memory, identity, and connection. To use time purely in service of financial efficiency is to flatten its value. An investor who spends their weekend fine-tuning a tax strategy may be intellectually engaged, but what are they postponing in the process? A walk with their child? A long, slow meal with someone they love? A conversation without agenda? These are not sentimental luxuries. They are the foundation of a meaningful life. And yet, they are often treated as optional, while financial tasks are treated as non-negotiable.

The irony is that many investors begin their financial planning with precisely these goals in mind: to spend more time with family, to travel, to write, to think freely. But somewhere along the way, the tools intended to serve those goals become goals in themselves. The process overtakes the purpose. The interface becomes more seductive than the life it was meant to support.

To reclaim autonomy from this pattern requires more than time management. It requires a reframing of what it means to be a good steward of wealth. *Good investing is not about doing more—it is about doing the right things less often and with greater intentionality.* This is where automation, delegation, and systems-based investing become not just practical solutions, but ethical ones. They free up attention. They reduce decision fatigue. They enable the investor to live a life that is richer not just in assets, but in experience.

Robo-advisors play a central role in this reframing. At their best, they are not simply algorithmic wealth managers. They are *infrastructure for reclaiming time.* They allow the investor to define parameters—goals, risk tolerance, values—and then release the need to monitor every fluctuation. They break the feedback loop that says more oversight equals more control. They enable a form of financial trust—both in the system and in oneself—that is foundational to living with clarity.

This trust is not blind. It is informed by data, history, and behavioural insight. The best-performing investors are rarely the most involved. Often, they are the ones who design systems they can walk away from. Fidelity once conducted an internal study to identify which clients had the best returns. The top performers? Those who had forgotten they had accounts. This is not a call for ignorance. It is a call for *strategic disengagement*—the recognition that sometimes, the smartest thing we can do is to step back.

This stepping back is not simply tactical—it is spiritual. Because when we step back, we begin to see more clearly what our money is actually for. Not just for retirement, or education, or protection, but for presence. For the ability to give attention freely, without constant mental tab-keeping. For the dignity of a life where every hour is not shadowed by a ticker. For the courage to say: *enough*.

In this light, time is not a by-product of financial success—it is its deepest expression. A well-structured, automated investment system is not a sign of laziness. It is a profound declaration that your life is worth living outside the confines of constant economic vigilance. That your mind deserves more than endless comparison charts. That your relationships deserve a version of you who is fully here.

The shift from accumulation to autonomy is subtle but transformative. It redefines wealth as the capacity to focus, to rest, to choose. It elevates peace of mind above marginal gains. It restores time to its rightful place—not as a means to optimise, but as the medium in which life unfolds.

This is the quiet crisis: not that we lack resources, but that we squander attention. Not that we fail to plan, but that we forget what we're planning for. To resolve this, we don't need better strategies. We need better priorities. And we need the courage to structure our financial lives around them.

Because the most precious asset you will ever have is not your net worth. It is the uninterrupted, unhurried experience of your own life. And no portfolio is worth more than that.

# Chapter 2
# What Robo-Advisors Really Are (And Why That Changes Everything)

Most people believe they already know what a robo-advisor is. A few taps, a neat dashboard with clever graphics, an algorithm humming invisibly in the background—and suddenly, your portfolio is "taken care of." At first glance, it's just another digital service: quick, cheap, efficient. Comparable, perhaps, to an online bank or a budgeting app. That description isn't wrong, but it is incomplete. Because the true significance of robo-advisors isn't in automation alone. It's in delegation—and not simply of tasks, but of authority, of identity, of trust itself.

What's unfolding with their rise is not just a shift in technology but a reorientation of philosophy: a reconsideration of how we relate to risk, decision-making, and money itself. These platforms unsettle long-standing assumptions—that real investors must stay hands-on, that effort and expertise are twins, that vigilance is proof of competence. Instead, they whisper a different story, one in which letting go is not weakness but wisdom. To grasp the meaning of robo-advisors, you have to peer past the code and screens, into the psychology they illuminate.

Delegation, after all, has long been a mark of maturity. Skilled leaders know when to pass the reins. Yet with money—especially the personal kind—outsourcing still carries a stigma. Automating feels like surrender; trusting a system feels like losing agency. There's an ingrained suspicion that handing responsibility to a machine must equal detachment. But this is a confusion of terms. It mistakes busyness for insight, and involvement for mastery. Robo-advisors, in their very design, refute that idea. They rest on the premise that consistency beats impulse, that a disciplined framework outperforms instinct, and that calm neutrality is far sturdier than adrenaline when it comes to wealth.

This inversion of the traditional creed is what makes them so quietly radical. Their disruption isn't in faster trades or slicker interfaces, nor in the replacement of humans with algorithms. It lies in the challenge they pose: to stop micromanaging. To release the illusion that tighter control produces better outcomes. For many investors raised on the gospel of "hands-on equals smart," this feels simultaneously liberating and unnerving.

Beneath the surface, these platforms are elegant engines. Most trace their intellectual roots to Modern Portfolio Theory, the framework crafted by Harry Markowitz in the 1950s that later won him the Nobel Prize in Economics. At its core, the theory argues for diversification—spreading investments across asset classes and calibrating their weights to match one's appetite for risk. The purpose is not clairvoyance, not picking tomorrow's winners, but balance: building portfolios that maximise expected return for any given level of risk. This isn't speculative fancy; it's the mathematical scaffolding that underpins institutional investing around the world.

Robo-advisors take that logic and operationalise it for the individual. They make accessible what once belonged to endowments, pension funds, and the well-advised wealthy—codifying it into systems that scale, that run quietly in the background, and that allow us, perhaps for the first time, to discover what happens when we step aside.

## Beyond the Interface: A Philosophy of Delegation

What if the greatest barrier to intelligent investing wasn't a lack of knowledge, but an inability to let go? Not of financial responsibility, but of the compulsive need to monitor, adjust, and optimise every decision? In the cultural imagination, investors are active agents—analysing markets, timing trades, outwitting volatility. But this archetype, still dominant in much of financial discourse, is not merely outdated. It's misleading. More than ever, the evidence suggests that *overinvolvement erodes performance.* And yet the resistance to delegation persists—not because it's irrational, but because it threatens something deeper than our wallets: our sense of control.

Robo-advisors challenge that resistance at its core. They appear, on the surface, to be simple tools—digital interfaces that allow individuals to automate their investments. But such a characterisation misses the point entirely. *They are not just software; they are behavioural infrastructure.* Behind the dashboards and algorithmic outputs lies a more radical proposition: that intelligent investing can emerge not from micromanagement, but from pre-commitment, trust in process, and the strategic minimisation of human error.

The rise of robo-advisors signals a shift not only in technology, but in financial philosophy. At the heart of this shift is the idea that *delegation is not the opposite of control, but a more sophisticated form of it.* Delegation, when well-structured, enables consistency. It frees the investor from emotional volatility. It separates decision from impulse. And perhaps most importantly, it redefines what it means to be engaged. To delegate wisely is not to disengage; it is to design systems that serve your intentions even when your emotions do not.

To appreciate this, one must first understand the cognitive and behavioural traps that plague most individual investors. The literature on behavioural finance is well-established: humans are predictably irrational. We anchor on irrelevant data. We overestimate our predictive power. We react to short-term volatility at the expense of long-term strategy. Loss aversion drives us to sell prematurely. Overconfidence leads us to tinker incessantly. And in an environment of 24-hour market updates, these tendencies are not only triggered—they're amplified.

Robo-advisors, by contrast, are indifferent to mood. They don't panic during a market dip. They don't chase performance. They don't suffer from narrative fallacy. They simply execute a pre-defined strategy, with rigour and without emotional distortion. This might sound cold or mechanical, but it's precisely this neutrality that makes them so powerful. *In a system dominated by human overreaction, consistency is a competitive advantage.*

Consider the act of rebalancing—a critical yet often neglected aspect of portfolio management. Most investors understand, in principle, that asset allocations should be periodically adjusted to maintain their intended risk profile. But in practice, rebalancing is emotionally counterintuitive. It requires selling outperforming assets and buying underperformers—exactly the opposite of what feels "right." A human investor hesitates. A robo-advisor does not. It acts on logic, not emotion. And that distinction, over years, has significant compounding effects.

This distinction becomes even more profound when we examine the psychological implications of automation. Delegating investment decisions to an algorithm confronts us with uncomfortable questions: *Do I really understand what I'm doing? Is my involvement actually improving my outcomes? Can I trust a system more than I trust myself?* These are not technical questions—they're existential ones. They force us to confront the myth of personal infallibility that underlies so much financial behaviour.

Many investors, especially those who pride themselves on being analytical, struggle with this confrontation. They equate knowledge with control, and control with security. To hand over decision-making to an algorithm can feel like an admission of defeat—or worse, irrelevance. But this reaction confuses ego preservation with effectiveness. The most successful professionals in any domain know that *leverage comes not from doing everything yourself, but from building systems that don't need your constant input.* In this light, using a robo-advisor is not an abdication of responsibility. It's an expression of mastery: the ability to step back and trust the architecture you've built.

The analogy to other domains is instructive. We do not manually calculate our GPS routes. We don't handwrite spreadsheets. We don't monitor the temperature of our ovens minute by minute. Instead, we design the input, and trust the system to execute the output. The wisdom lies in the setup—not in the constant tweaking. And yet, when it comes to investing, many people behave as if every market shift demands a new decision. Robo-advisors reject this premise by design. They impose *structural patience.* They convert intention into action, and insulate that action from the noise of the moment.

This insulation is not a weakness. It is precisely what enables alignment. Because if the goal of investing is not to "win" the market—but to build long-term financial independence, peace of mind, and time freedom—then the metrics that matter are not beating benchmarks, but *staying invested, staying consistent, and staying sane.* Robo-advisors are built to serve these metrics. They don't just move money. They create distance—between reaction and decision, between fear and behaviour, between distraction and direction.

And yet, despite these advantages, the adoption of robo-advisors still carries a stigma in some circles. They are often viewed as tools for the financially unsophisticated, or for those too lazy to learn. But this view is outdated and misinformed. Today's most sophisticated investors—from tech entrepreneurs to behavioural economists—are increasingly embracing automated systems, not because they lack skill, but because they understand that *discipline is a stronger edge than cleverness.* Delegation, in this context, is not a concession. It is a strategy.

Take, for example, the widespread use of automated trading systems in institutional finance. Hedge funds, pension funds, and sovereign wealth managers use algorithmic strategies because they remove bias, execute consistently, and scale efficiently. The same principle applies in the retail context. The only difference is that robo-advisors democratise that capability—offering the rigour of institutional logic to everyday investors, without the overhead or complexity.

The elegance of this model lies in its architecture. A user inputs their risk profile, time horizon, and financial goals. The system constructs a diversified portfolio based on modern portfolio theory, periodically rebalances to maintain alignment, reinvests dividends, and—on more advanced platforms—optimises for tax efficiency. But beneath this mechanical flow is a behavioural scaffolding. Every feature is designed not just to execute, but to *reduce the behavioural tax* that individual investors so often impose on themselves.

This behavioural dimension is easy to overlook because it's invisible. There's no dashboard that shows how many bad decisions you avoided. But those avoided decisions—those non-events—are often the most valuable outcome. The trade not made. The panic not acted on. The performance-chasing scheme not followed. In this sense, robo-advisors are not just financial tools. *They are anti-distraction devices.* They help investors remain aligned to their highest-level intentions, rather than getting lost in the day-to-day turbulence of market activity.

The broader philosophical implication is this: investing, at its best, is not about control. It's about clarity. The clarity to define what matters, to design a system around those priorities, and to step out of your own way. Delegation is how that clarity becomes durable. It's what allows your financial life to operate quietly, effectively, and in the background—so that your attention can return to the foreground of living.

To see robo-advisors only as financial widgets is to miss their significance. They represent a shift from personality-driven investing to process-driven investing. From hero narratives to system narratives. From performance obsession to behavioural optimisation. They are not replacements for wisdom. They are vehicles for implementing it.

The decision to use a robo-advisor, then, is not a shortcut. It is a choice. A choice to trust a system over a mood. To trust decades of data over the story in your head. And to value peace of mind as a legitimate return on investment.

It is, in the end, a philosophy—a deliberate and mature recognition that sometimes, *the smartest thing you can do with your money is to stop trying to control it so tightly*. And let the system you've chosen do what it's been built to do.

## The Algorithms Behind the Curtain

When people think of robo-advisors, their attention often lands on the surface: the clean interfaces, the pie-chart dashboards, the sliders adjusting risk tolerance from "conservative" to "aggressive." It's a user-friendly experience, and deliberately so. But beneath that polished exterior lies a deeply sophisticated system—one shaped by decades of academic research, mathematical modelling, and behavioural finance. What distinguishes robo-advisors from their human counterparts is not simply cost or convenience. It's the way they operationalise proven investment principles at scale, with rigour, consistency, and—most crucially—without ego.

At the core of most robo-advisors sits a theoretical framework that emerged in the 1950s: Modern Portfolio Theory (MPT), developed by economist Harry Markowitz. For this work, Markowitz would go on to win the Nobel Prize in Economic Sciences. The insight was deceptively simple: the performance of an investment portfolio is not determined solely by the characteristics of its individual components, but by the way those components interact. In technical terms, risk is not additive. A well-diversified portfolio can offer higher expected returns for the same level of risk—or less risk for the same return—simply by optimising the correlation between asset classes. This concept transformed investment management from a series of isolated choices into a structured discipline of allocation.

What makes MPT so foundational to robo-advisors is its formalisation into algorithms. Rather than relying on human intuition or prevailing market narratives, robo-advisors use quantitative models to design portfolios that maximise expected return per unit of risk—typically measured as standard deviation. The process begins with input: the investor's goals, time horizon, risk appetite, and in some cases, values or preferences (such as ESG considerations). These inputs become the parameters for optimisation. The algorithm then constructs a portfolio composed of diversified assets—usually a mix of low-cost ETFs across domestic and international equities, bonds, and sometimes alternative assets—designed to deliver the best possible trade-off between risk and return.

But the power of robo-advisors is not just in their initial construction. It is in their ongoing calibration. One of the most common causes of underperformance among human investors is poor timing—buying high, selling low, chasing trends, or reacting emotionally to volatility. Robo-advisors solve for this through automated rebalancing. As market movements push the allocation out of sync—say equities surge and become overweight in a balanced portfolio—the algorithm sells down the outperforming assets and reallocates to underperformers, restoring the original risk profile. This process, while mechanical, reflects a principle that's extraordinarily difficult for humans to follow: *discipline without bias*.

To appreciate this fully, consider what happens during a market correction. A human adviser might talk a nervous client through their fears, invoking historical data, reminding them of long-term goals, perhaps offering a mild adjustment to restore confidence. But a robo-advisor doesn't engage in persuasion. It acts. It executes the rebalancing, regardless of sentiment, with no deviation based on narrative or opinion. In this context, automation isn't cold—it's consistent. It doesn't negotiate with fear. It adheres to structure.

This distinction is critical because it removes one of the greatest liabilities in investing: the investor. Behavioural finance has repeatedly demonstrated that investors often underperform their own investments. That is, the funds themselves generate stronger returns than the people who invest in them, simply because people enter and exit at suboptimal times. By outsourcing not just the trades but the timing and discipline, robo-advisors provide a form of *behavioural guardrailing*. They are not merely financial instruments—they are decision protocols that protect the investor from themselves.

To see this in action, look at the data. Numerous studies comparing robo-advised portfolios to those managed by individuals show not only better net returns (thanks to lower fees and fewer mistakes), but also reduced volatility in investor experience. The investor who delegates to a system is less likely to panic in a downturn or chase performance during a bull market. Instead, they maintain alignment with a strategy that reflects their long-term objectives. This psychological stability has real financial consequences. Staying invested is more powerful than timing correctly once or twice.

But the elegance of these algorithms lies not in their complexity—it lies in their humility. Robo-advisors are not built to forecast market direction. They don't claim to predict which sectors will surge or which geopolitical event will trigger a downturn. They don't trade on hunches or attempt to generate alpha through stock-picking. Instead, they assume that markets are broadly efficient, that diversification is the only free lunch, and that time in the market beats timing the market. These are not flashy insights, but they are resilient ones. And critically, they avoid the overconfidence that plagues human-led investing.

Some critics argue that this model is too static—that it lacks the nuance of human judgment or the flexibility to respond to unique market conditions. But this critique overlooks a central point: *the greatest risk to long-term investing is not market complexity, but behavioural inconsistency*. Humans are inconsistent. Systems are not. And the best robo-advisors are not rigid—they are rules-based with adaptive parameters. Many incorporate drift thresholds, tax-loss harvesting triggers, or dynamic asset allocation models that respond to structural changes over time. The difference is that these changes are encoded, not improvised.

Take, for instance, the way advanced robo-advisors integrate tax efficiency. Algorithms monitor portfolios for opportunities to sell declining assets at a loss (to offset capital gains), while simultaneously purchasing similar but not identical assets to maintain exposure. This process—tax-loss harvesting—requires vigilance, precision, and unemotional timing. It is prohibitively difficult for most individuals to implement manually, but for a well-coded system, it is standard protocol. The result is an invisible but meaningful improvement in after-tax returns—without the investor needing to lift a finger.

At a deeper level, the algorithmic core of robo-advisors challenges the myth that good investing requires constant adjustment. We are culturally conditioned to believe that involvement signals competence, that watching the markets closely is synonymous with being a "responsible" investor. Robo-advisors invert that assumption. They suggest that intelligence is better expressed through system design than through constant activity. That your value lies not in how often you act, but in how clearly you define the rules by which your money should be managed.

This is not to say that all robo-advisors are created equal. There are meaningful differences in fee structures, asset selection, customisability, and underlying models. Some are strictly rules-based; others offer hybrid solutions with access to human advisers. Some integrate factor-based investing or smart beta strategies, layering in additional complexity. But what unites them is the *removal of ego*. They don't trade to prove a point. They don't need to be right. They're not driven by reputation or client expectations. They are built to serve the strategy, not to deviate from it.

In many ways, this is their greatest contribution: not just better investing, but *cleaner investing*. Investing without stories, without bias, without the need to be seen as clever. Investing that starts with a clear goal and works backward—not forward from market headlines. Investing that is less performative, more rational, and more sustainable.

For the intelligent investor, the allure of robo-advisors is not that they do everything for you. It's that they do the right things *without you*. They allow you to design a plan and step back—knowing that what's happening behind the curtain isn't magic, but method. What the algorithms offer is not omniscience, but structure. And in a domain where structure beats brilliance more often than we care to admit, that is a deeply underrated virtue.

## When Machines Become Mirrors

Delegating your investments to a machine seems, on paper, like a technical decision—an optimisation of effort, cost, and time. You input your risk profile, answer a few questions about your goals, and a clean algorithm takes care of the rest. The interface is frictionless, the process efficient. Yet for many people, the real hesitation isn't about fees, data security, or even performance. It's psychological. The act of handing over control to a system—particularly a silent, impartial, unflinching one—creates discomfort not because we doubt the system, but because it reflects truths about ourselves we'd rather not confront.

A robo-advisor, at its best, is unemotional. It follows rules. It ignores noise. It rebalances systematically, harvests tax losses opportunistically, and holds steady through turbulence. It's not built to be clever; it's built to be consistent. And that consistency, while desirable in theory, challenges a deeply human narrative: *that good investing is a test of intelligence, competence, and personal insight.* When a machine performs better than we do—precisely because it doesn't care about being clever—we're forced to re-evaluate not just our strategy, but our self-concept.

This is where delegation ceases to be a purely functional act and becomes an existential one. Because what we delegate, in effect, is not just the task of asset management. We are delegating our right to intervene. We are outsourcing the opportunity to prove ourselves, to assert control, to express identity through decision-making. And for many, that loss feels more profound than the risk of underperformance.

The reluctance to automate is often rationalised as prudence: "I like to keep an eye on things." "I trust my instincts." "I enjoy being hands-on." But beneath these surface-level explanations is frequently something more vulnerable: *a discomfort with surrender.* We've been conditioned to equate control with intelligence, effort with virtue, and complexity with mastery. In this context, stepping back doesn't feel like efficiency—it feels like irrelevance. If I'm not actively doing something with my money, am I being responsible? Am I even still the kind of person who takes their future seriously?

This discomfort is especially pronounced among high-achieving individuals. Professionals who excel in their careers often bring a performance-oriented mindset to their investments. They're used to being evaluated on outcomes, rewarded for effort, and recognised for insight. Financial decision-making becomes another stage on which to perform competence. So when an algorithm quietly outperforms them—not by being smarter, but by doing less—they experience not just cognitive dissonance, but identity disruption.

Take the example of Anjali, a senior consultant at a global strategy firm. With an MBA from a top-tier school and a keen interest in economics, Anjali had always managed her own investments. She enjoyed researching sectors, adjusting allocations, and discussing financial strategies with peers. Her returns were inconsistent, but the activity felt affirming. When she transitioned part of her portfolio to a robo-advisor at the recommendation of a colleague, she found herself checking it compulsively—less out of concern than out of discomfort. She wasn't used to not being the expert. When the robo-portfolio outperformed her manually managed one over 18 months, she didn't feel vindicated. She felt diminished. What did it say about her skills if the better strategy was to walk away?

Anjali's reaction is not unusual. Many people interpret financial delegation as a threat to their intellectual self-worth. In a culture where knowledge and control are tightly bound to status, the idea that *less involvement might lead to better outcomes* feels counterintuitive.

Yet this is precisely what behavioural finance teaches us: most individual investors are not punished for ignorance; they are punished for overconfidence. The human brain, for all its brilliance, is poorly designed for probabilistic, long-term decision-making. We react emotionally, chase patterns that aren't there, and feel compelled to act when inaction would serve us better. In this landscape, the machine is not smarter—it's *less compromised.*

And that's what makes it a mirror.

When we hand control to a machine that doesn't need ego validation, we come face to face with the extent to which our financial behaviour has been driven by ego. When we see that automated discipline outperforms our informed tinkering, we're forced to admit that we weren't being rational—we were being performative. The machine doesn't just outperform us; it humbles us. And that humility is uncomfortable precisely because it's clarifying.

But there is also a deeper opportunity here—because when we confront the need to always be the one in control, we get the chance to *redefine what control really means*. If the ultimate goal of investing is not status, not mastery, but freedom—freedom of time, freedom of thought, freedom to live according to one's values—then the obsession with intervention is not a strength. It's a liability. The question becomes: *what do I need to let go of in order to get what I truly want?*

This reframing allows us to see robo-advisors not as technological substitutes, but as *behavioural companions*. Their design compensates for our cognitive biases. Their unemotional consistency gives us space to step away from performative decision-making. Their quiet, rule-based operation gives us a model for what self-trust might look like when decoupled from control. In delegating to the system, we are not diminishing our agency—we are refining it. We are choosing to design the game rather than constantly trying to play it.

The irony is sharp: by giving up our need to manage every variable, we gain a kind of mastery that is deeper, quieter, and more sustainable. It's the mastery of designing a system that reflects our actual priorities—and then trusting it enough to let it work. That trust is not automatic. It requires a maturity that few financial institutions talk about: *the maturity to accept that you are not your returns, not your clever trades, not your portfolio performance.* You are the designer of the system, not its hero.

This shift is especially liberating for those who have conflated financial activity with moral responsibility. Delegating doesn't mean you don't care. It means you care enough to choose the approach most likely to deliver your goals—and then redirect your attention to what matters most. When machines take over what doesn't need your genius, you're left with the space to apply your genius where it *does* matter: your work, your relationships, your learning, your creativity. In this context, delegation is not loss—it's alignment.

There will always be those who find comfort in manual control. And for some, the process of managing their investments is genuinely fulfilling. But for many others, that control is performative, compulsive, or simply inherited. It's not about outcomes; it's about reassurance. And when they delegate, they are forced to ask: *Who am I when I'm not proving myself through financial control?*

That question, uncomfortable as it is, lies at the heart of modern investing. Not because we need to become passive, but because we need to become *intentional.* The machine doesn't strip us of identity—it invites us to stop outsourcing it to volatility. It invites us to define ourselves not by how closely we track the market, but by how clearly we track our own values.

When machines become mirrors, they reveal our deepest assumptions about control, security, and competence. But they also offer a way through. They show us that trust is not the absence of diligence—it is the result of it. They remind us that real intelligence is not about doing everything yourself. It's about knowing what to hold, what to let go, and what to automate. And that sometimes, the most profound insight doesn't come from mastering the system—but from stepping away from the screen, confident that the system is doing what you designed it to do.

## Not Just for "Lazy Investors"

One of the most enduring misconceptions about robo-advisors is that they are designed for people who can't be bothered to learn about investing. The narrative suggests that automation is a crutch for the disengaged, the under-informed, or the financially indifferent. In this framing, handing your portfolio to an algorithm is akin to submitting your taxes without checking the numbers, or outsourcing your health to a fitness app without understanding your own physiology. It implies passivity, if not outright negligence. But this caricature does not hold up under scrutiny. The reality is far more nuanced—and far more intellectually interesting.

Robo-investing is not about laziness. It is about *leverage*. It reflects a growing recognition among strategic thinkers that the most important resource in modern life is not money, but attention. In a world saturated by demands on our time, the smartest investors are not those who work hardest to beat the market, but those who design systems to achieve their goals with the least cognitive friction. These are not passive investors in the lazy sense—they are *active delegators*, choosing clarity and automation not out of ignorance, but from a place of principled design.

This distinction is often misunderstood because traditional investing culture has long valorised hustle. The archetype of the serious investor is still shaped by the imagery of Wall Street: multiple monitors, endless data, rapid-fire decisions, CNBC humming in the background. Activity is mistaken for insight, and hands-on involvement is conflated with effectiveness. But this assumption is belied by a growing body of evidence from behavioural finance, which consistently shows that frequent trading, emotional reactivity, and overconfidence are the main drivers of underperformance.

It is within this behavioural context that robo-advisors offer a radical alternative. They are not tools for those who don't care. They are tools for those who *do* care, but who want to allocate their care intelligently. By building portfolios based on long-term principles—diversification, risk-adjusted returns, disciplined rebalancing—robo-advisors take care of the most important things, leaving investors to focus their energy on the parts of life that actually require human creativity, judgement, and presence.

Consider the mindset of a strategic minimalist. This is someone who doesn't try to do everything, but who ensures that what *is* done is of high quality and aligned with their goals. They are not disengaged—they are discerning. In the context of finance, this means understanding that effort is not always rewarded and that constant vigilance does not guarantee better outcomes. Strategic minimalists are willing to do the work of *thinking through a system once*, so they don't have to think about it constantly. They value simplicity, not as a default, but as a discipline.

This distinction becomes especially relevant in high-performance environments. Many professionals—consultants, surgeons, designers, academics—operate in fields that demand their full attention. They know how to work hard, and they know what deep work requires. For them, spending hours rebalancing a portfolio or reading speculative commentary is not a badge of honour. It is a misallocation of cognitive bandwidth. Delegating these tasks to a system is not an act of evasion. It is an intentional preservation of mental energy for where it is most needed.

Take the case of Tariq, a senior engineer at a leading tech firm. He has a graduate degree in computer science, strong quantitative skills, and a deep understanding of markets. For years, he managed his own portfolio, rebalancing quarterly and obsessively reading financial news. But as his professional responsibilities grew and he started a family, he realised that his personal investing habits were consuming time and attention that could be better spent elsewhere. Switching to a robo-advisor didn't reflect a lack of ability—it reflected a shift in priorities. He was no longer trying to *win* at investing. He was trying to *opt out* of the illusion that he had to.

This shift is emblematic of a broader change in the psychology of investing. The old model placed the investor at the centre of every decision. It rewarded hypervigilance and constant involvement. The new model removes the ego from the equation. It recognises that the most valuable decisions are often the ones you make *once*, and then design around. By trusting a system to execute those decisions consistently—without emotional distortion—you liberate yourself from the exhausting treadmill of always needing to do more.

This is not passivity. It is a form of *meta-engagement.* The decision to delegate is itself an act of design. It reflects a view of the world in which intelligence is not demonstrated by direct manipulation, but by *structural foresight.* Delegating to a robo-advisor is no different from using automation in business operations or relying on checklists in aviation. It does not imply detachment. It implies a belief that consistency beats improvisation—and that automation can be a tool for expressing clarity, not avoiding it.

And yet, despite this sophistication, the stigma persists. The myth of the "lazy investor" endures in part because it flatters those who remain immersed in the game. It reinforces the cultural belief that hard work is always superior to smart systems. But the data says otherwise. Study after study shows that automated, passive strategies outperform most actively managed portfolios over time. The reason is not technical. It is behavioural. Humans are tempted by stories, susceptible to overreaction, and often terrible at recognising their own biases. Machines are not better because they are smarter. They are better because they are *simpler*, and they don't deviate from the plan.

This reframing is essential. Robo-advisors are not a way of avoiding responsibility—they are a way of redefining it. They allow investors to take responsibility for the things they *can* control—like how much risk they want to take, what goals they are saving for, and how often they want to review their strategy—while outsourcing the parts that don't require daily human judgement. They convert intentions into systems. And in doing so, they allow investors to get on with their lives.

It's important, then, to ask a different set of questions. Not "Is this too easy?" or "Am I being irresponsible by automating?" but rather: *What do I really want my financial life to do for me? Where do I want to spend my time and attention? What does it mean to design a system I can live with—not just during bull markets, but during inevitable downturns?*

These are not questions that a lazy investor asks. They are the questions of someone who is deeply engaged with what matters most—*not just the mechanics of wealth accumulation, but the design of a life that is thoughtful, focused, and aligned with their values.*

To dismiss robo-investing as simplistic is to misunderstand what sophistication really looks like. It is not found in the number of trades made, or the complexity of a portfolio. It is found in *clarity of intention, quality of process, and discipline of execution.* And in that respect, strategic minimalism is not the absence of effort. It is the highest form of it.

Those who embrace automation are not avoiding the work. They are choosing *better work*. Work that requires human presence, creativity, and moral agency. Work that cannot be delegated to an algorithm. They are not less responsible for their finances—they are more responsible with their attention. And in a world where noise is endless and urgency is manufactured by default, that is not laziness. It is wisdom

# Chapter 3
# The Case for Intelligent Surrender

The financial world rarely sits still. Markets buzz with speculation, investors chase headlines, forecasters warn of downturns, and every app on your phone tempts you to "check in," as though vigilance alone were a wealth-building strategy. Beneath this swirl lies a quiet presumption: that doing more must mean doing better. That the investor who tweaks portfolios most often, reacts the quickest, hustles the hardest, will inevitably win. Yet history, data, and behavioural science point in the opposite direction. In investing, effort does not reliably produce excellence. In fact, it often corrodes it.

This chapter is an invitation to rethink what financial intelligence really means. Not intelligence in the narrow sense of technical mastery or fluency in market jargon, but a subtler kind: emotional intelligence. The discipline to hold back when restraint serves you best. The humility to live with uncertainty without leaping at every shadow. The maturity to align with systems deliberately designed to be steadier, calmer, more rational than we are on our own. Intelligent surrender is not abdication of control. It is a redefinition of it.

Decades of research point in one direction: passive, broadly diversified portfolios have outperformed the bulk of actively managed funds over the long haul. Vanguard's numbers suggest that about four in five active mutual funds lag their benchmarks after fees across ten years—and the longer you extend the timeline, the starker the failure. This isn't because fund managers lack skill. It's the structural drag created by incessant decision-making: transaction costs, timing errors, cognitive blind spots, and the ceaseless pressure to perform, even when markets themselves are stagnant or turbulent. Put simply, the more you do, the more you invite error. In investing, patience is not passivity. It is strategy.

But this truth rubs against the grain of cultural conditioning. From an early age we're told to hustle, to stay vigilant, to intervene before it's too late. Investing, then, becomes another theatre of performance, where self-worth is bound to the illusion of control. Fintech apps with their glossy dashboards, financial news cycles that loop endlessly, and the romanticised figure of the lone stock-picker all feed this belief. Behavioural finance, however, exposes its flaws with merciless clarity. Our brains are ill-equipped for the calm, probabilistic reasoning that long-term investing demands. We are wired to panic, to overweight recent events, to flee losses faster than we chase gains.

Loss aversion, articulated by Daniel Kahneman and Amos Tversky, shows why investors dump assets in downturns despite sound fundamentals. The pain of losing £1,000 stings twice as much as the pleasure of gaining it. Overconfidence convinces individuals they're natural-born market timers or stock-picking prodigies—despite the evidence stacked against them. Recency bias magnifies the last market hiccup into a grand prophecy. These aren't anomalies; they're baked into human nature. Modern platforms, with their real-time feedback loops, only amplify the damage.

Which is why automation enters the scene not as a novelty but as an antidote. Robo-advisors don't attempt to outsmart the market. They aim to outbehave it. Their algorithms carry out what most humans can't sustain: methodical diversification, unemotional rebalancing, efficient tax strategies, and relentless cost control. They don't doomscroll newsfeeds. They don't panic in sell-offs. Most crucially, they enforce inaction when action would be most destructive—a discipline almost impossible to self-enforce when fear or greed takes the wheel.

At first, allowing a machine to steward your investments can feel unnervingly like irrelevance. For investors who equate financial engagement with competence, surrendering the driver's seat is disorienting. But discomfort is not always danger. Sometimes it signals growth. Delegating to a system is not retreat. It is recognition: a conscious acknowledgement of where human judgement excels and where, left unchecked, it sabotages.

This shift is more philosophical than technical. Traditional finance conditions us to optimise everything—returns, tax, fees, timing. Intelligent surrender shifts the lens. It asks: what if optimisation meant emotional resilience, freedom of time, and alignment with values? What if success were not about besting the market, but about enduring long enough to let compounding quietly perform its alchemy? What if the goal weren't superiority over peers but sustainability of one's own path?

That reframing alters everything. It places the spotlight not on tactical ingenuity but on behavioural fit. Many strategies glisten in spreadsheets yet disintegrate in lived reality—they demand too much attention, too much reactivity, too much psychic cost. By contrast, a strategy tuned to temperament—automated, rules-based, quietly consistent—becomes not just effective but tolerable. And tolerance, often overlooked, is the bedrock of staying power. The best portfolio is not the one with the highest projected return. It's the one that keeps you invested when your instincts scream to flee.

Here lies the heart of intelligent surrender: a move from control to curiosity. By abandoning the urge to second-guess every cycle or predict every shift, you create space for better questions. Not "What's the market doing this week?" but "Does my system still serve my goals?" Not "Should I react?" but "What is fuelling this urge to act?" Curiosity becomes resistance—a subtle act of defiance against the anxiety-soaked culture of constant performance.

Ironically, relinquishing control in markets hands you greater control over yourself—your time, your energy, your serenity. You stop tethering your worth to portfolio graphs and begin measuring it by how effectively your system supports your larger life. You evolve from jittery speculator to thoughtful architect.

Take Michelle, for instance, a 41-year-old founder of a sustainable fashion label. After years spent tinkering with her allocations, scanning commentary, and stressing over market chatter, she hit a wall. Her relentless effort wasn't producing better results; it was merely siphoning time and creativity she longed to invest in her business. Moving to a robo-advisor, for her, was less about disengagement than about dignity. It freed her to channel energy from financial noise into strategic growth, from spreadsheet fatigue into creative flow. Her portfolio became steadier, yes—but more importantly, it grew quieter. And that quiet, she says now, felt like wealth.

This framing matters. The true purpose of investing isn't the thrill of the chase or the pride of outperforming neighbours. It is freedom—freedom from stress, from emotional whiplash, from the relentless drain of hyper-involvement. Intelligent surrender doesn't lower the bar. It raises it—demanding that investments repay us not just with returns, but with clarity, ease, and peace of mind.

Letting systems outthink you is not capitulation. It is alignment. It recognises that real intelligence is not always in perpetual action, but in design—and in the restraint to let that design breathe. It is the wisdom to know that some of the best financial decisions are the ones you decline to revisit weekly. It is the quiet assurance that the strongest structures are often the ones you can forget about.

Within these pages, you'll see the data that upholds this philosophy, the stories that flesh it out, and the tools that make it practicable. But above all, you'll be offered a new lens: investment not as theatre, but as foundation. Not as puzzle, but as practice. Because often, the most intelligent move you can make with your money is to stop trying to outwit it—and allow it, patiently, to work.

## Why Doing Less Can Outperform Doing More

The most expensive mistakes in investing often come wrapped in the illusion of productivity. Checking your portfolio daily. Timing trades. Jumping between asset classes based on market whispers. Scanning headlines for macroeconomic "clues." These activities *feel* industrious, even strategic. But beneath this surface-level activity is a sobering truth: the majority of individual investors would do far better by doing far less. Not because they aren't smart enough to engage with the markets, but because the markets don't reward that kind of engagement. They punish it.

The evidence is both deep and durable. Numerous long-term studies conducted across multiple market cycles have consistently shown that passive, rules-based investing outperforms the vast majority of high-effort strategies over time. A 2022 SPIVA (S&P Indices Versus Active) scorecard revealed that over a 20-year period, more than 90% of actively managed US large-cap funds underperformed their benchmark. And it's not just about fees. It's about *behaviour.* Active investors tend to trade too often, respond too emotionally, and systematically misjudge risk.

This isn't a moral critique. It's a behavioural diagnosis. Human brains are not naturally wired to make sound investment decisions in noisy, volatile environments. We are evolutionarily predisposed to see patterns where none exist, to react strongly to loss, and to seek short-term resolution to long-term uncertainty. The act of doing more in investing—more checking, more reallocating, more reacting—is typically an expression of psychological discomfort, not strategic advantage.

What's particularly striking is how this overactivity contradicts our behaviour in other domains of long-term strategy. A seasoned architect does not re-edit blueprints mid-construction. An experienced pilot does not grab the manual controls during every gust of turbulence. Yet in finance, investors are taught—explicitly or tacitly—that constant input equals control, and that control equals returns. The data disagrees.

One of the more influential studies to demonstrate this was conducted by Brad Barber and Terrance Odean at the University of California. After examining the trading records of over 60,000 households, they found that the most active traders underperformed the least active ones by a wide margin. Their research revealed a clear pattern: excessive trading was not driven by superior insight, but by overconfidence and reaction to short-term market noise. The investors who made fewer moves—and stuck to broad, diversified portfolios—retained more capital and experienced fewer psychological shocks.

The deeper insight here is that effort, in financial markets, is not linearly correlated with reward. This is hard for many high-achieving professionals to internalise. In most other fields—medicine, engineering, law, academia—working harder and learning more typically translates into better outcomes. In investing, the reverse is often true. The more you try to "beat" the market, the more likely you are to underperform it.

This runs directly against the prevailing hustle ethos that dominates modern financial culture. Social media, investment forums, and financial influencers have created an ecosystem where activity is equated with seriousness. Platforms reward commentary and prediction, not discipline. Algorithms favour bold claims, not evidence. As a result, a warped version of investing has taken hold—one that sees success as the product of tactical brilliance rather than behavioural alignment.

But long-term investing isn't a game of brilliance. It's a test of consistency. That's why simple, rule-based portfolios tend to outperform: they sidestep the investor's worst impulses. A globally diversified index fund portfolio, rebalanced periodically, may appear underwhelming compared to the sleek interfaces and custom allocations of more "sophisticated" approaches. But its power lies in its insulation—from human error, from emotional distortion, and from the siren song of market noise.

Take, for instance, the experience of endowment funds managed by large universities. The top-performing funds over multi-decade horizons tend to have remarkably stable asset allocation strategies. Their performance isn't the result of hyperactive trading desks but of disciplined, evidence-based policy adherence. The lesson here isn't that you need a billion-dollar investment committee. It's that when incentives are aligned toward stability—not reaction—returns tend to follow.

To understand why doing less works so consistently well, it helps to revisit the concept of compound interest. Compounding is the most powerful mechanism in investing—but it is also the most fragile. Its power unfolds slowly, requiring time, consistency, and minimal interruption. Active strategies often interrupt this process. A poorly timed market exit—even one or two misjudged moves—can derail years of compounding. The true cost of overactivity is not just the loss of returns; it's the forfeiture of future exponential growth.

That forfeiture also takes a psychological toll. Constant involvement in markets can lead to decision fatigue, second-guessing, and unnecessary stress. Many investors confuse motion with mastery, only to find themselves trapped in a loop of anxiety and regret. Doing less, by contrast, cultivates a kind of emotional neutrality. It fosters resilience, not through willpower, but through design. Systems-based investing—especially when automated—removes the need to constantly decide. And removing the need to decide is, in practice, a form of liberation.

There's also a moral dimension to consider. Time spent obsessing over market minutiae is time not spent elsewhere—on relationships, creativity, community, or health. An investing strategy that requires constant attention is, by definition, one that costs attention. Strategic minimalism is not just efficient; it is *ethical.* It asks: how much of your life should your money take from you in order to preserve or grow itself?

This question gains urgency in light of recent trends. The gamification of investing, particularly among younger demographics, has turned market speculation into a form of entertainment. Apps like Robinhood have blurred the lines between trading and digital dopamine. But beneath the sleek UX and confetti graphics lies a troubling reality: these platforms profit from overactivity. They reinforce a loop in which users are nudged toward more trades, more risk, more short-term thinking. The result? A generation of investors learning the hard way that doing more often delivers less.

Passive investing is not about disengagement. It is about structured restraint. It is a conscious rejection of the myth that constant action yields superior outcomes. It is a commitment to discipline over drama, evidence over instinct, and time-tested principles over trending narratives. It asks the investor to step out of the performance cycle and into a posture of stewardship—where the goal is not to outmanoeuvre the market, but to participate in its growth with humility and patience.

Of course, doing less doesn't mean doing *nothing*. It means doing the *right* things, at the *right* time, for the *right* reasons. It means selecting a strategy grounded in sound financial theory, aligned with your goals and temperament, and revisiting it only when your life—not the market—changes in meaningful ways. It means choosing process over prediction.

Ultimately, the question is not whether you can beat the market. Some investors do, some don't. The real question is whether trying to beat the market is worth the time, energy, and psychological cost it extracts. For most people, most of the time, it isn't. That's not cynicism. That's design. It's recognising that the best outcomes in investing often belong not to the most active minds, but to the most disciplined ones. And discipline, in practice, looks like this: less input, fewer moves, more trust in the system you built.

There is a quiet power in that kind of trust. It doesn't scream on trading floors or flash on financial news tickers. But over decades, it speaks loudly through balance sheets and bank statements. It's the power of doing less, and getting more—not by accident, but by design.

## The Illusion of Control in Markets

Control is a seductive idea. It reassures us, flatters us, and sells easily. It suggests that outcomes can be bent to will, that complexity can be tamed with enough attention, and that mastery over uncertainty is not only possible—but expected. Nowhere is this illusion more persistent, or more damaging, than in the world of investing. Investors, particularly those with education, resources, and confidence, often overestimate their ability to predict, manage, or outperform markets. Yet time and again, both the data and human psychology offer the same lesson: our instincts betray us, and our sense of control is often just that—a sense, not a skill.

At the heart of this behavioural misalignment are two of the most well-documented cognitive biases in financial psychology: *loss aversion* and *overconfidence bias*. Together, they form the architecture of false control—driving us to act when we should observe, to trade when we should wait, and to double down when we should stand back.

Loss aversion, first formalised by Daniel Kahneman and Amos Tversky through Prospect Theory, describes the asymmetric way we experience financial outcomes: the pain of losing £1,000 is psychologically more powerful than the pleasure of gaining it. It's not a mild preference—it's a distortion. People are estimated to feel losses roughly twice as intensely as gains of equivalent size. In market contexts, this leads to erratic, often destructive behaviour: clinging to declining assets in the hope of recovery, panic-selling during corrections, or prematurely exiting a position that momentarily dips below purchase price. The instinct is not rooted in logic, but in emotional miscalibration. It is, at its core, an attempt to *regain control* of an outcome we fear has escaped us.

Now layer overconfidence on top of that. Overconfidence bias—our systematic overestimation of our abilities, knowledge, or influence—fuels the belief that we can out-think, out-manoeuvre, or out-predict a system as vast, complex, and chaotic as global markets. Academic studies have shown that most investors believe they are above-average—a statistical impossibility—and routinely rate their own decision-making as superior to others'. This is not a marginal error. It's foundational. It shows up in everything from excessive trading (which data links to underperformance) to the refusal to use automated tools that statistically outperform manual ones.

Consider the case of individual day traders, particularly during periods of heightened market excitement. In 2021, for instance, a wave of new retail investors surged into markets via apps like Robinhood, emboldened by social media momentum and low-cost access. Many were convinced they had special insight or timing. But studies later showed that the majority underperformed benchmarks and incurred significant losses—despite spending hours monitoring charts, engaging in forums, and making high-frequency trades. Their problem wasn't ignorance. It was misplaced confidence. They mistook involvement for expertise, and activity for advantage.

Institutional investors are not immune. A famous analysis by Dalbar Inc. has for years documented the so-called "behaviour gap": the discrepancy between average investment returns and the actual returns realised by investors. The culprit is not the market—it's investor behaviour. Even professional fund managers, with advanced models and access to proprietary data, have struggled to beat the market after fees. When the illusion of control is baked into strategy, underperformance follows. Repeated attempts to time exits and entries, chase alpha, or hedge against rare events too often result in unnecessary complexity and higher costs.

But why is this illusion so hard to shake?

Partly because financial markets present themselves as puzzles to be solved. We're given constant streams of data—charts, earnings reports, forecasts, geopolitical updates—all of which *suggest* that the more you watch, the more you'll understand. Yet the majority of this information is noise, not signal. The market digests new information in milliseconds. By the time a retail investor "acts" on a headline, the professionals have already moved. What remains is an afterimage—a ghost of a signal that feels actionable, but isn't.

This environment encourages what behavioural economists call *narrative bias*: the tendency to impose a coherent story on random or ambiguous data. Investors often link their decisions to a story that explains their action—"Tech is the future," "This stock is undervalued," "I had a good feeling." But these stories are often retrofitted rationalisations, not causes. The narrative gives a comforting illusion of intentionality, masking the randomness underneath.

It is here that robo-advisors present a quiet revolution. Their logic is not reactive, but rule-based. They do not "believe" they can beat the market. They assume they can't. And rather than chasing control, they focus on reducing its most damaging side effects. By automating asset allocation, rebalancing, tax optimisation, and long-term strategy execution, robo-advisors remove the investor's temptation to over-steer. And that, paradoxically, yields better results—not just financially, but emotionally.

When you no longer believe that market outcomes depend on your next move, your mindset shifts. You stop checking prices daily. You ignore irrelevant headlines. You don't interpret volatility as failure. You return to your actual life. *This isn't laziness. It's alignment.* It reflects a clear-eyed understanding of where control ends and where process begins.

There are, of course, exceptions. Some professional investors do consistently outperform—though they are rare, and often operate under very different constraints than individual investors. But for most people, the pursuit of control in markets leads not to success but to suffering: anxiety, regret, wasted hours, and missed compounding. The antidote is not withdrawal, but recalibration.

The investor who understands this doesn't relinquish responsibility. They redefine it. They choose frameworks over forecasts. They prioritise resilience over reaction. And they measure progress not by their ability to anticipate headlines, but by their ability to follow through on strategy—even when it's boring.

This reframing demands courage. Letting go of the belief that you are in control is deeply uncomfortable, especially in cultures that reward confidence and hustle. But in investing, as in aviation, surgery, or chess, mastery often means knowing when *not* to intervene. The best pilots do not fly the plane manually during turbulence. They let the autopilot do what it's built to do.

That's not passivity. It's precision.

When markets lurch, as they inevitably do, the investor gripped by the illusion of control will ask: *What should I do?* The investor who has let go of that illusion will ask: *Is my system still aligned with my purpose?* That's a better question—and over decades, it leads to better answers.

## Letting Systems Be Smarter Than You

If intelligence is the ability to make good decisions in the face of uncertainty, then the modern investor must confront an uncomfortable truth: *systems are often better decision-makers than we are.* Not because they are perfect, but because they are less emotional, more consistent, and structurally immune to many of the cognitive traps that plague human judgement. When we allow systems to guide our investing behaviour, we are not surrendering control—we are upgrading it. We are choosing reliability over reactivity, discipline over instinct, and structure over improvisation.

This is a hard sell in a culture that lionises mastery, intuition, and gut feeling. Much of the rhetoric around investing—especially in its more active forms—glorifies the idea of personal brilliance. Think of the archetypal trader: fast, alert, reading signals in real-time, making bold moves under pressure. The implicit message is clear: *you must be smarter than the market to win.* But this mythology, while cinematic, is rarely supported by evidence. The data tell a very different story. Over decades, it is not the most active, most confident, or most informed investors who tend to perform best—it is those who establish a sound system and stick to it, especially when it's hard.

Consider the performance of passive index funds versus actively managed funds. The SPIVA (S&P Indices Versus Active) scorecards, published regularly by S&P Dow Jones Indices, consistently show that the majority of active fund managers underperform their benchmarks over longer periods—despite access to cutting-edge research, teams of analysts, and constant market surveillance. The conclusion is both simple and sobering: the more one tries to beat the market by timing entries and exits or picking stocks, the lower the odds of long-term outperformance.

But the issue runs deeper than outcomes. It cuts into how we perceive risk, reward, and our own role in the investing process. Humans are not wired for consistency. We are subject to mood swings, news cycles, biases, blind spots, and the ever-present temptation to "do something"—especially when faced with volatility. This behavioural vulnerability undermines even the most well-intentioned strategies. A well-crafted plan can be derailed not by bad data, but by a single impulsive decision made during a market dip.

Systems, on the other hand, do not flinch. A well-designed algorithm, especially one embedded in a reputable robo-advisor platform, does not panic during a sell-off. It does not overreact to headlines. It does not chase hot stocks or second-guess its own logic. It simply executes the strategy it was programmed to follow: rebalancing, allocating, harvesting tax losses, and keeping the investor aligned with their risk profile. And that quiet consistency, over time, compounds into performance.

This is not to say that systems are immune to error. No model can predict black swan events, and no algorithm can guarantee positive returns. But the core advantage of automation lies not in clairvoyance—it lies in *discipline.* Automated systems enforce behavioural consistency. They remove the investor from the cockpit during moments of turbulence, allowing the plan—not the panic—to dictate the next move.

One of the most misunderstood aspects of automation in finance is the fear that it diminishes agency. Critics argue that relying on robo-advisors, model portfolios, or rebalancing algorithms amounts to outsourcing one's financial future to a machine. But this misframes the issue. Delegation is not abdication. It is, in fact, a higher form of responsibility. It requires the investor to make a fundamental strategic choice: *do I trust a well-researched, mathematically coherent system to act on my behalf, or do I believe that I can consistently outthink a trillion-dollar global marketplace?*

Let's consider this through the lens of aviation. Modern planes are equipped with sophisticated autopilot systems capable of handling nearly all phases of flight. The pilot is not rendered useless—they are still responsible for takeoff, landing, and high-level oversight—but they are no longer expected to manually control every degree of movement at every second. This has not led to a decline in safety; quite the opposite. Automation in aviation has significantly reduced human error, the single largest cause of crashes. The best pilots understand that their job is not to override the system, but to understand when and how to intervene when the system requires it.

The same principle applies to investing. When systems are well-calibrated—when they are built on sound financial principles, properly risk-adjusted, and aligned with long-term goals—they should be trusted to run without constant interference. The investor's role becomes less about micro-decisions and more about macro-design: selecting the right framework, defining their risk appetite honestly, and ensuring that their personal values are reflected in their financial configuration.

Behavioural economists have long understood that humans overestimate their ability to manage complexity. The *illusion of control* bias leads us to believe that effort and involvement equate to mastery. We think that checking our portfolio daily, reading financial news obsessively, or reacting swiftly to market swings makes us smarter investors. But often, it makes us worse. Nobel laureate Richard Thaler, a pioneer in behavioural finance, once remarked that many investors would be better off if they simply looked at their accounts less frequently. The reason is psychological: the more we watch, the more we react, and the more we react, the more likely we are to abandon our plan at precisely the wrong time.

This is where automation becomes not just a tool, but a safeguard. A behavioural scaffold. A form of cognitive offloading that frees us from the burden of unnecessary vigilance. In an age where attention is fragmented, energy is finite, and stress is ubiquitous, intelligent automation offers a kind of mental hygiene—it protects us from ourselves.

Take the example of tax-loss harvesting, a technique used by many robo-advisors to enhance after-tax returns. It involves selling securities at a loss to offset taxable gains, then reinvesting the proceeds in similar assets to maintain portfolio exposure. When done manually, this requires detailed tracking, careful timing, and a strong stomach. Most investors either do it poorly or not at all. But when automated, it becomes an invisible advantage—executed silently, rationally, and without emotion.

Another case is dynamic rebalancing. Portfolios drift over time. Left unattended, they can gradually accumulate risk or veer away from target allocations. Rebalancing corrects this drift. But few investors have the discipline to rebalance at precisely the right moments—usually because rebalancing feels counterintuitive. It often involves selling winners and buying underperformers, which goes against our natural inclination to chase momentum. Algorithms, unburdened by these impulses, rebalance with clinical precision. The result is not perfection, but discipline—delivered at scale.

What we're seeing is a reframing of investor intelligence. It's no longer about who can predict the market better. It's about who can design a system they trust—and then stay out of its way. In this model, success is measured not by clever trades or timely exits, but by *alignment*—between values, strategy, and behaviour.

This shift can be confronting. It challenges long-held beliefs about self-reliance, expertise, and the virtue of effort. But it also offers something rare in the modern financial world: *peace of mind.* When you trust the system, you sleep better. You stop measuring your worth by your most recent investment decision. You begin to live your life in the foreground again—while your portfolio runs quietly, intelligently, in the background.

Ultimately, letting systems be smarter than you is not about giving up. It's about choosing your battles wisely. It's about recognising where your judgment adds value—and where it introduces noise. And it's about having the humility to admit that, sometimes, the smartest move is to let go.

## From Control to Curiosity

One of the most quietly radical questions an investor can ask themselves is: *What if I stopped trying to win?* Not in the defeatist sense of giving up, but in the intellectual sense of releasing the need to outperform others, predict the unpredictable, or constantly validate one's intelligence through markets. What if investing wasn't a contest—but a design exercise? What if success was measured not by outperformance, but by coherence—between your strategy and your psychology?

This reframing is more than philosophical. It addresses a central dysfunction in modern investing: the fixation on control. We are told, implicitly and explicitly, that good investors are active investors. That the disciplined are the ones who lean in, monitor relentlessly, and intervene at the right moment. That intelligence in finance means outmanoeuvring randomness. Yet this idea often produces the opposite of wisdom. It turns investing into a struggle, fuels anxiety, and breeds emotional decision-making in the name of rationality.

Behavioural finance offers us a more accurate view. Decades of research—pioneered by scholars like Daniel Kahneman, Amos Tversky, and Richard Thaler—demonstrate that our brains are not naturally suited to financial decision-making. We are prone to loss aversion, overconfidence, hindsight bias, confirmation bias, and dozens of other distortions that compromise our judgement. And paradoxically, the more we believe we are in control, the more vulnerable we become to these invisible forces.

Shifting from control to curiosity begins with the recognition that markets are not puzzles to be solved. They are systems of complex, interdependent behaviour—driven by variables that exceed any individual's capacity to process in real time. The fantasy of mastery, of perfectly timing entries and exits or consistently identifying undervalued assets, is seductive because it appeals to our desire for agency. But it often becomes an expensive illusion. Not just financially, but psychologically.

By contrast, curiosity invites a different mindset—one grounded in inquiry rather than conquest. It asks: *What system could I design that I'd be willing to follow—not just when the market is calm, but when it's collapsing? What level of volatility am I emotionally prepared to tolerate? What does "enough" look like for me, and how do I build toward it without self-sabotage?* These questions move investing out of the realm of ego and into the domain of self-awareness.

This shift has deep practical consequences. It means, first and foremost, that investing becomes less about optimisation and more about tolerability. A strategy that produces the highest theoretical return is meaningless if it's also the one you're most likely to abandon in a downturn. Conversely, a slightly less "efficient" strategy that you can follow calmly and consistently may yield better outcomes simply because you stick with it. *Emotional sustainability beats intellectual perfection.*

Take, for example, the difference between a highly leveraged tactical strategy and a diversified, passive portfolio designed for long-term compounding. The former may produce impressive returns in bull markets, but it demands constant vigilance, an appetite for drawdowns, and a level of time commitment that erodes attention from other areas of life. The latter, by contrast, offers no daily thrills—yet it preserves energy, reduces cognitive load, and allows life to remain in the foreground. For the curious investor, this raises a deeper question: *what kind of life am I optimising for?*

One of the least discussed virtues in investing is *non-reactivity*. The ability to hold a position, ignore the noise, and avoid the temptation to tinker is not a sign of apathy—it is a signal of maturity. This becomes even more powerful when supported by systems that reinforce calm behaviour, such as robo-advisors, pre-set rebalancing thresholds, and automatic contributions. These tools are not shortcuts for the lazy—they are instruments for the curious. For those who care less about outperforming and more about understanding their own limits.

This mindset change also reorients our definition of success. Instead of comparing performance to an abstract benchmark—or to peers, pundits, or historical data—the curious investor looks inward. They ask: *Did I act in alignment with my values? Did I protect my attention? Did I make choices I can live with, even in retrospect?* These questions are both more difficult and more relevant than "did I beat the market?"—because they recognise the emotional and temporal context in which investing decisions are made.

A concrete illustration of this philosophy is found in the FIRE (Financial Independence, Retire Early) movement, particularly among those who practise its more sustainable offshoots. Many adherents choose simplicity over complexity—not because they can't handle volatility, but because they prefer autonomy. They optimise for freedom, not maximisation. They automate their savings, limit their exposure to unnecessary financial products, and build in buffers that protect them from reacting emotionally to short-term market moves. Their strategies are often elegant in their restraint. And restraint, here, is not a limitation—it's a feature.

This approach is especially relevant in a digital age saturated with noise. The average investor now has access to more information, more platforms, and more opinions than ever before. Yet this abundance rarely translates into clarity. Often, it does the opposite.

It overwhelms, distracts, and provokes action when stillness would be more profitable. Curiosity helps us see through this fog. It allows us to ask: *Which data actually inform my decision-making? Which metrics matter to me? What inputs am I better off ignoring altogether?*

Importantly, this is not a call for passivity. It is a call for *selectivity*. For making fewer, more thoughtful decisions. For building a system that reflects what matters most to you—not what impresses others or optimises spreadsheets. It is the difference between being in control and being in contact: with your goals, your values, and your tolerances.

The final, and perhaps most transformative, shift is this: curiosity creates space for growth. When investing is no longer a scoreboard, it becomes a sandbox. You are free to explore without fear. To experiment modestly, within boundaries. To learn from mistakes without spiralling into regret. This psychological safety is crucial—because, ultimately, the quality of your decisions will be shaped less by what you know, and more by how you relate to uncertainty.

Letting your strategy breathe means accepting that you are not supposed to have all the answers. It means designing something strong enough to weather storms and simple enough to live with. It means resisting the pressure to intervene at every market hiccup—and trusting that the absence of action is often the most intelligent choice available.

So what happens when we stop trying to beat the market? We gain something far more valuable: peace with it. We let go of the illusion of control, and in its place, we cultivate agency. We recognise that wisdom isn't found in predicting the next turn—it's found in building a vehicle we trust, fastening our seatbelt, and choosing roads that align with the kind of journey we want to have. Not exciting. Not heroic. But profoundly liberating.

# Chapter 4
# Designing Your Wealth Autopilot

The most consequential financial decision you'll ever make may not arrive with fanfare. It's unlikely to occur in the drama of a market crash or the thrill of a sudden windfall, but rather in a quiet moment when you resolve to build a system that runs without you. Wealth, so often imagined as the product of constant hustle, daring trades, and endless optimisation, has another path. This chapter argues for that alternative: that the most transformative move isn't an adrenaline-fuelled grind, but a once-off act of design. Not you managing money each day, but a system constructed to manage you.

This isn't an airy idealism. It is the practical promise of modern robo-advisors: carefully configured systems that allow your capital to grow unobtrusively, guided by your values rather than your impulses. But "set and forget" is only as wise as the setup itself. Too often, people treat it superficially—clicking defaults, accepting risk scores at face value, ticking boxes like it's a formality. What follows is not strategy but autopilot of the shallowest kind. What's needed instead is a deeper act: treating investment setup not as a digital product interaction but as the architecture of a personal future.

Robo-advisors, after all, are not monolithic. They are cultural artefacts as much as technical tools, shaped by the philosophies of their creators. Betterment leans into design elegance and goal-visualisation. Vanguard embodies legacy trust and the gospel of low-cost indexing. Nutmeg highlights its hybrid of algorithmic efficiency with a human hand in the loop. In India, Scripbox contextualises investment within cultural norms of long-term family wealth. These are not just feature lists; they are philosophies in code. Choosing among them is as much about finding alignment with your own values as it is about performance metrics.

Yet even the best-designed platform cannot fix a more subtle mismatch: the gap between your stated tolerance for risk and the reality of it. Digital onboarding has a blind spot here. People misstate their risk appetite—not always intentionally, but because they misunderstand it. They answer as they wish to be, or as they think they ought to be. A 30% drawdown may look tolerable in theory, but when the decline is real, fear often overwhelms resolve. This is not weak character. It's a lack of self-awareness, intensified by questionnaires that reduce human complexity to neat categories.

This chapter invites you to look harder at those nuances. Instead of neat labels, it offers prompts, stories, and exercises that map the emotional landscape of risk: where fear resides, where bravado hides, where calm can be trained. A sustainable investing system requires more than financial literacy; it demands behavioural honesty. We'll explore how tolerance shifts with age and circumstance, why regret minimisation often trumps return maximisation, and how to build a design resilient enough to hold you steady through inevitable storms.

Then there is the matter of goals. Most robo-advisors ask you to label them: "retire at 55," "buy a home," "save for education." These are placeholders masquerading as plans. They sound tidy, but they lack weight. This chapter challenges you to press deeper—what does "retiring early" truly mean? Is it freedom of place? The chance to reinvent yourself? A shield against burnout? Vague goals generate vague strategies. Goals that feel alive, rooted in emotion, generate clarity—and that clarity cascades into allocation, risk calibration, withdrawal strategy.

This is the moment when design becomes more than functional. When your system reflects the truth of your life, not the abstraction of a spreadsheet, it transforms into something larger than a portfolio. It becomes a container for your future self. And the act of building it—carefully, consciously—becomes an act of radical alignment. You are not just arranging investments; you are installing guardrails, buffers, and values into the very infrastructure of your financial life.

And here is the startling part: the whole configuration, if approached with clarity, need not consume more than an hour. One focused hour in which you make decisions that reverberate for decades. From there, automation takes over: contributions flow, portfolios rebalance, tax harvesting occurs in the background, glide paths shift with age. What remains with you is not the ceaseless labour of tinkering, but the quiet role of steward. You cease being an anxious micromanager and become instead a deliberate architect.

It's worth dwelling on how sharply this contrasts with the old paradigm of finance. The traditional model celebrates complexity, rewards novelty, and flatters the illusion that attention equals control. Here, the argument is its opposite: that a well-built wealth system frees attention, rendering it precious rather than perpetually demanded. And with that freedom comes the chance to redirect energy toward pursuits more vital: creativity, relationships, a life measured by time rather than ticks of a market chart.

Of course, automation isn't free from psychological friction. The fear of missing out. The dread of permanence. The ego's discomfort at stepping back. These resistances are not technical—they are personal, almost existential. For many, investing has become a surrogate for agency and identity. To release the reins feels like diminishing oneself. Yet what it really marks is a shift—from performance for its own sake to purposeful restraint. That shift is possible only when the system you've built is sturdy enough to deserve your trust.

This chapter will walk that road with you. Not with generic product reviews, but with practical exercises to align platforms with your values. Not with shallow risk labels, but with tools for genuine behavioural reflection. Not with placeholders for goals, but with prompts that tie them to your lived aspirations. And finally, a sample walkthrough to illustrate how, in practice, you might configure your own wealth architecture—not for a tick-box, but for endurance.

You don't need encyclopaedic market knowledge to do this well. You don't need to forecast GDP or memorise ticker codes. What you do need is honesty, intentionality, and a willingness to invest a quiet hour in the design of something that might serve you for forty years. That is not abdication; it is leadership of the highest order. Leadership that liberates you from the exhausting myth that wealth must always be chased.

This is the promise of financial autopilot—not the erasure of responsibility, but its redefinition. A system built so faithfully around your values that it does the heavy lifting for you. Not flawlessly. Not magically. But steadily, quietly, intelligently—so you can live your life, not just bankroll it.

## Choosing the Right Robo for Your Values

The choice of a robo-advisor is rarely framed as a matter of personal philosophy. Most comparison tables focus on fees, asset allocations, and performance metrics. These are important, of course, but they only tell part of the story. Choosing a robo-advisor is not unlike choosing a business partner or a therapist: you are selecting a system to which you will entrust your attention, your earnings, your anxieties, and your long-term hopes. And yet, most people make the decision based on a homepage colour scheme, a few screenshots, or the promise of "zero fees for six months." This article argues for a more thoughtful approach—one that begins with values, not just variables.

At its core, a robo-advisor is a set of algorithms wrapped in a user interface, underpinned by a worldview about money, risk, and the role of technology. Every platform embodies choices made by its designers: about what to automate, what to leave manual, what to visualise, and what to hide. These choices are not neutral. They reflect assumptions—about investor psychology, about optimal behaviour, about trust. To choose a robo-advisor wisely, you must learn to read between the lines of features and find the design philosophy beneath. Are you being encouraged to interact frequently, or step back? Does the language frame investing as conquest or stewardship? Does the interface make you feel empowered or overwhelmed? These are not superficial UX considerations—they are windows into the ethos of the product itself.

Consider Betterment. Founded in the wake of the 2008 financial crisis, Betterment was built on the belief that emotional investing destroys wealth and that automation can act as a behavioural buffer. Its tone is minimalist, calm, and confidence-inspiring. Betterment encourages goal-based investing, gently nudging users to define life objectives—retirement, education, major purchases—and maps portfolios to those timelines. There is a deliberate absence of adrenaline. The app rarely prompts you to intervene. It doesn't reward hyper-attention. It trusts that if the system is set up well, it should mostly run itself. For investors seeking emotional insulation from market volatility, this is a deeply aligned environment.

Wealthfront, by contrast, appeals to a slightly different temperament—still rational, but more optimisation-driven. It speaks the language of financial engineering. Its value proposition is grounded in tax efficiency, direct indexing, and smart cash management. Wealthfront's interface is sharp, data-rich, and intellectually reassuring. It assumes a user who wants to understand the machinery under the hood without getting greasy. This is a platform that attracts engineers, consultants, and analysts—those who don't necessarily want to manage their portfolio manually but want to *understand* that it's being managed with rigour. The cultural tone is one of intelligent leverage: don't just automate—*automate well.*

Then there is Vanguard Digital Advisor—a natural extension of the brand that pioneered index investing. Where Betterment and Wealthfront feel like startups, Vanguard feels like a financial public utility. Its philosophy is rooted in long-termism, cost minimisation, and behavioural patience. Vanguard doesn't seduce with interface design or digital polish. Instead, it offers quiet competence, backed by decades of client trust. For investors who prize legacy, transparency, and the dignity of unflashy wealth-building, Vanguard delivers a kind of comfort that no modern fintech veneer can replicate.

Nutmeg, the UK-based robo-advisor, brings yet another tone into the mix. Positioned between boutique investment service and fully digital platform, Nutmeg offers discretionary management alongside algorithmic portfolios. It understands that British investors often value bespoke advice and are wary of fully handing control to code.

Nutmeg's language blends confidence with caution, appealing to those who want modernity with a human fallback. Its interface is cleaner than a traditional wealth manager's portal, but more conservative than Silicon Valley startups. Nutmeg reflects a distinctly British sensibility: *trust the system, but verify through dialogue.*

Scripbox, a leading robo-advisory platform in India, contextualises investing within a vastly different cultural and regulatory landscape. Indian households are often first-generation equity investors, deeply conservative, and heavily influenced by family narratives and real estate bias. Scripbox positions itself not just as a tool, but as an educator. Its onboarding flows are conversational and pedagogical. Its dashboards favour simplicity over sophistication. And its messaging speaks to *trust-building in transition*—from traditional saving habits to modern portfolio-based thinking. It recognises that automation is not merely a convenience here—it is a bridge between the old world of fixed deposits and the new world of market exposure.

What these examples show is that robo-advisors are not just differentiated by technical capabilities, but by cultural cues. They encode assumptions about the user—what you fear, what you value, how much cognitive load you want to carry, and how emotionally resilient you are in the face of market turbulence. This is why selecting a platform requires more than just reading a feature list. It requires a kind of *self-assessment*—not just "what do I want to invest in?" but "how do I want to relate to money, attention, and decision-making?"

It also requires ethical discernment. Few investors think to ask: *How does this platform make money?* Does it profit from my inactivity, my reactivity, or my long-term growth? Is its fee structure transparent, or layered with obscured incentives? Does it recommend its own products under the guise of impartiality? These are not paranoid questions—they are baseline due diligence. In a landscape where zero-commission investing often conceals order flow monetisation, understanding the *economic model behind the interface* is essential. A robo-advisor should not only align with your financial goals, but with your ethical boundaries.

This brings us to usability philosophy. Some platforms assume their users want control with training wheels. Others assume you want to surrender completely. Some prompt frequent re-engagement. Others shield you from volatility updates. Your selection should align with your desired cognitive posture. If you're a chronic tinkerer trying to build discipline, a platform that minimises notifications and discourages dashboard visits may be more valuable than one that offers rich analytics. If, on the other hand, you're confident in your behavioural restraint, but crave transparency, a more data-forward platform might serve you better.

This is a quiet but profound decision. You're not just selecting an app. You're selecting a *frame*—a frame that will shape how you think about investing, how often you intervene, and what stories you tell yourself about progress. Your choice will influence your emotional bandwidth, your sense of agency, and your relationship to effort. And because the default human tendency is to engage too much, not too little, the right robo-advisor can be a form of *structural correction*—a gentle counterbalance to the behavioural biases we've explored earlier in this book.

To be clear, no platform is perfect. There will always be trade-offs between cost, customisation, transparency, and design. But what matters is *alignment.* When your chosen robo-advisor reflects your values—around money, autonomy, attention, and simplicity—it ceases to be just a product. It becomes a system you can trust, and perhaps more importantly, a system you can *forget.* Not in the sense of neglect, but in the sense of confidence. You don't wake up wondering if your investments need micromanagement. You've already done the hard work of selection. Now the system does the work of continuity.

That is the promise of intelligent delegation. And it begins not with knowing the right answer, but with asking the right questions: What kind of investor am I, not in theory, but in practice? What kind of guidance do I respond to—data, encouragement, silence? Where does my anxiety show up, and how can design help regulate it? What does "ethical investing" mean to me, and does my platform honour that definition?

These are not questions that robo-advisors can answer for you. But they are questions that the *right* robo-advisor can honour, accommodate, and support. This is not a trivial selection. It is the scaffolding for your future behaviour—and, by extension, your future wealth. Choose accordingly.

## How to Set Risk Profiles Without Lying to Yourself

There's a peculiar moment that recurs at the beginning of every investment journey: the investor, when prompted by a sleek digital form or a well-meaning advisor, is asked to describe their own tolerance for risk. It's a question that sounds simple, even empowering. But behind its surface lies a psychological trap: we rarely answer with honesty. Instead, we answer with aspiration, delusion, or projection. We don't say who we are—we say who we think we *should* be. And that, more than any market event or economic cycle, is what derails long-term financial outcomes.

Risk tolerance questionnaires are ubiquitous. Most robo-advisors—regardless of how advanced their backend algorithms may be—begin with this crude sketch: How would you feel if your portfolio dropped by 20%? Are you more focused on growth or stability? What's your investment time horizon? These are not poor questions per se. The problem is that we answer them in a vacuum—detached from lived experience, filtered through ego, optimism bias, and social comparison. It's easy to say "I'm comfortable with high volatility" when the markets are calm and the answers are hypothetical. But real risk tolerance is not a belief—it's a behaviour under stress.

Take the case of Andrew, a 41-year-old software architect who began investing through a robo-advisor in 2018. When he filled out his onboarding survey, he selected the "aggressive growth" portfolio. He had a stable income, no debt, and a long time horizon. He understood market cycles. On paper, it was a logical choice. But when the pandemic-triggered crash arrived in March 2020, Andrew panicked. He pulled his investments out at a 28% loss—right before the rebound began. He later admitted that despite having "read all the right blogs" and "knowing it would recover," he couldn't stomach the red numbers. His self-assessed risk profile had been aspirational. His actual risk profile was something quite different.

This gap between stated and actual tolerance is not a personal failing. It's structural. Behavioural economists have shown time and again that humans are poor predictors of their future emotional states. This is especially true in contexts involving uncertainty, loss, and social pressure. *Affective forecasting*—the process by which we estimate how we'll feel in future scenarios—is notoriously flawed. We underestimate how much market downturns will affect our mood, our confidence, and our sense of agency. Conversely, we overestimate our ability to stay rational and detached.

Loss aversion compounds the problem. As Daniel Kahneman and Amos Tversky famously demonstrated, we feel the pain of losses roughly twice as intensely as we feel the pleasure of equivalent gains. This creates a distortion: even if a portfolio performs well over time, the temporary drawdowns feel disproportionately punishing. Investors often claim they're long-term thinkers until they actually lose money—then the timeline shrinks, and panic sets in. The rational calculus of compound interest collapses under the weight of emotional immediacy.

So how does one set a risk profile that reflects reality rather than fantasy? The first step is to move from *projection* to *observation*. Instead of asking "What kind of risk-taker do I want to be?", start by asking, "How have I responded to financial uncertainty in the past?" Reflect on specific instances: How did you react during the 2008 crisis? What did you do when the market dropped in early 2020? Did you feel compelled to check your account daily? Did you act, freeze, or tune out? These moments hold more insight than any hypothetical questionnaire ever could.

Second, replace abstract questions with embodied simulations. One useful exercise is to imagine your portfolio drops 30% overnight. Not in theory—imagine it as if it happened *this morning*. What's your immediate urge? Do you want to sell everything? Do you feel calm but vigilant? Or do you begin researching news stories and seeking explanations? Your visceral response is data. Some platforms now use "stress tests" that show users the historical volatility of their chosen asset mix. But it's not the chart that matters—it's what you *feel* when you see that chart.

There's also a social dimension to risk that's often ignored. Investors don't operate in a vacuum. Our risk preferences are shaped—sometimes warped—by the narratives we absorb from friends, colleagues, and media. Consider the investor who reads about a friend's crypto windfall or a colleague's aggressive tech stock bets. Even if they intellectually believe in index funds and long-term stability, the ambient social pressure can distort their self-perception. They begin to feel "too conservative," not because their needs have changed, but because comparison has eroded clarity. The antidote is intentional solitude: build your risk profile in silence, not in the noisy theatre of others' highlight reels.

Moreover, it's critical to distinguish between *risk tolerance* and *risk capacity*. Tolerance is emotional—how much volatility you can stomach. Capacity is structural—how much volatility you can *afford* based on your financial situation. A 28-year-old freelancer with no dependents may tolerate high volatility but have low capacity if their income is unstable. A 60-year-old with a secure pension may have low emotional tolerance but high capacity. Many people conflate the two, resulting in portfolios that are misaligned not just emotionally, but mathematically.

Robo-advisors, to their credit, are beginning to grapple with these nuances. Some platforms now offer dynamic risk assessment tools that monitor behaviour over time—how often you log in, whether you withdraw during market dips, and how you respond to automated nudges. These behavioural breadcrumbs are far more predictive than initial survey responses. A user who claims to be high-risk but checks their portfolio daily and reacts to short-term headlines is sending a clear signal: their stated tolerance doesn't match their lived temperament.

Another approach is narrative anchoring. Instead of describing yourself with terms like "conservative" or "aggressive," describe the *story* you want your money to tell. Are you building quiet stability, or chasing exponential growth? Are you seeking peace of mind, legacy, optionality? Risk then becomes a function of alignment. A portfolio that's volatile but consistent with your personal narrative may feel less stressful than one that's "safe" but inauthentic. *Clarity reduces anxiety more effectively than conservatism.*

For readers ready to confront their real tolerance, here are a few prompts worth engaging with—privately or with a partner:

– When was the last time I lost money, and how did I react?
– Do I equate risk with recklessness or with opportunity?
– Am I trying to prove something with my portfolio—or am I trying to provide for someone?
– What does "safety" mean to me? Is it about capital preservation, emotional stability, or not feeling foolish in front of others?
– If I had to explain my investment decisions to my future self, would I sound thoughtful or performative?

These are not typical financial questions. They are psychological, even existential. But they cut closer to the truth than any 10-question form could.

Ultimately, the goal is not to eliminate risk, nor to perfectly calibrate it. The goal is *self-congruence.* A portfolio built on inaccurate assumptions about your risk tolerance is not just inefficient—it's dangerous. It invites overreaction, poor timing, and emotional dissonance. By contrast, a portfolio aligned with your temperament may not maximise theoretical returns, but it will maximise *durability.* And durability—your ability to stick with a system over time—is the real engine of compounding.

In the age of automation, this honesty becomes even more vital. Robo-advisors are only as effective as the inputs they receive. Garbage in, garbage out. If you misrepresent your risk tolerance, even the most elegant algorithm cannot save you. But if you bring clarity, humility, and self-awareness to the process, the system becomes not just efficient, but profoundly humane. It reflects who you are—not who you're pretending to be.

And that, perhaps, is the most radical outcome of financial technology: not just that it manages money well, but that it *invites self-knowledge* along the way.

## Don't Just Optimise—Humanise Your Goals

Ask an average investor why they're saving, and the answers will sound familiar: *retire early*, *buy a house*, *financial freedom*, or *just grow my wealth.* These phrases are repeated so often they've become the ambient soundtrack of modern finance. But dig a little deeper—ask what *retire early* means in practice, what *freedom* feels like on a Tuesday morning, or what kind of house they hope to live in—and you'll encounter a disconcerting pause. The truth is that most financial goals, as stated, are vague to the point of abstraction. They're not goals. They're slogans. And no algorithm, no matter how elegantly optimised, can chart a meaningful path toward a destination that hasn't been properly imagined.

Robo-advisors are designed to simplify complexity. But simplicity without context can become superficial. A portfolio allocation strategy that optimises for risk-adjusted returns is useful—*if* it's anchored to something emotionally true. The problem is that many investors bring empty language to the table. They input placeholder goals into sleek interfaces, ticking boxes for "moderate risk" or "long-term growth," without ever asking the harder question: *What is this money really for?* Not just in a logistical sense, but in a deeply human one. Until that question is answered, all optimisation is premature.

Consider a real-world example. Priya, a 38-year-old marketing consultant, set up a robo-advisor account with the goal of "retiring by 55." The platform dutifully suggested a portfolio based on her age, income, and risk tolerance. It looked sophisticated. But Priya hadn't thought through what retirement meant to her. Did she want to stop working entirely? Was she aiming to travel, volunteer, or launch a passion project? Did she need £40,000 per year—or £100,000? Was she assuming her health would hold up? These distinctions matter. A vague desire to "retire early" yields one kind of portfolio. A well-articulated vision of life at 55 yields another—possibly with different liquidity needs, asset allocations, or savings rates.

*Optimising without humanising leads to portfolios that look good on paper but feel hollow in practice.*

So how does one humanise a financial goal? Start by abandoning the language of finance, at least temporarily. Don't begin with asset classes, drawdown risk, or Monte Carlo simulations. Begin with memory and imagination. Ask: What are the moments you're trying to afford? Who are you with? What does the day look like? Where do you wake up? What constraints no longer define your life? These narrative anchors allow you to reverse-engineer the numbers with more precision and less emotional guesswork.

The most powerful financial goals are not numerical. They are *visceral.* They make your future self feel closer, more familiar. "Retire with £2 million" is a sterile target. "Have breakfast in my garden every day with no emails and no commute" is a design principle. One invites comparison. The other invites commitment.

Let's examine the idea of *financial independence*, a buzzword popularised by the FIRE movement (Financial Independence, Retire Early). At its best, it's a call for intentional living. But too often, it becomes performative—another race, this time toward early exit. Many FIRE adherents optimise savings rates aggressively, trimming every expense, pushing for lean retirement. The spreadsheets are beautiful. But behind the curtain, burnout often brews. They've optimised the numbers—but not the *why* behind the numbers. Humanising the goal might mean acknowledging a desire for part-time work, community, creative freedom, or mobility—not just escaping the office forever.

There's also a cultural layer worth naming. In many societies, money is a proxy for status, competence, or safety. This makes it harder to articulate goals honestly. People say they want a house—not because they crave homeownership, but because it's expected. They say they want "generational wealth"—not because they have a vision for legacy, but because it signals seriousness. *Much of financial goal-setting is contaminated by borrowed aspirations.* Robo-advisors can't detect this misalignment. Only deep reflection can.

Humanising your goals also means *accepting trade-offs.* A plan that funds annual travel and early retirement may not leave room for a private school education. A desire to live off passive income may mean tolerating slower lifestyle upgrades. When goals are clear, these trade-offs feel like strategy. When goals are vague, they feel like loss. Clarity transforms constraint into design.

One helpful exercise is to name your financial goals in tiers: essentials, enrichments, and indulgences. Essentials are non-negotiable—housing, healthcare, stability. Enrichments improve quality of life—travel, flexibility, creative time. Indulgences are bonuses—luxury items, second homes, legacy giving. This framework does not reduce ambition. It contextualises it. It allows you to design a portfolio that reflects your priorities with nuance, not noise.

Automation can help—but only after human goals are clearly defined. For instance, a user who specifies that they want to take a sabbatical every five years will have different liquidity requirements than one aiming to build long-term passive income. A robo-advisor can optimise for that, but only if it's told what to optimise *for*. Otherwise, the system defaults to generic templates—useful, but insufficient.

There's also a psychological reward to humanised planning: *it makes discipline easier*. Investors who are emotionally connected to their goals are more likely to stay the course during volatility. When the market dips, a vague goal like "build wealth" offers little comfort. A specific one—"buy land for my parents' retirement in Kerala"—offers ballast. It turns numbers into meaning.

Furthermore, humanised goals allow for evolution. As life unfolds, desires shift. Children are born. Careers change. Illness intervenes. A well-constructed financial plan is not rigid. It adapts. But it adapts best when its foundations are not just technical, but personal. Investors who have taken the time to articulate *why* they invest are more agile when their *how* needs to change.

It's worth noting that some robo-advisors are beginning to integrate behavioural coaching into their platforms. Rather than just managing assets, they're prompting users to revisit goals annually, to simulate trade-offs, and to visualise outcomes. This is a welcome development. But the technology is only as good as the self-awareness it assumes. *Automation amplifies intent. It does not replace it.*

Humanising your goals is not a one-time exercise. It's a reflective practice. Just as you rebalance your portfolio, you should periodically rebalance your priorities. What once felt urgent may no longer matter. What once seemed indulgent may now feel essential. By revisiting your goals with openness—and refining them with specificity—you bring your financial life into alignment with your lived values.

Ultimately, money is not the goal. Nor is optimisation. The goal is a life that feels meaningful, stable, and expressive of who you are. Financial tools, including robo-advisors, are scaffolding for that project. But the blueprint must come from within. *Don't just input numbers into systems. Input intent.*

When you humanise your goals, your investment plan becomes more than efficient. It becomes coherent. Not just mathematically—but emotionally, ethically, and personally. And that coherence, more than any market performance metric, is the true foundation of financial wellbeing.

## A Setup that Takes One Hour—and Changes Decades

There's a peculiar irony at the heart of modern investing: people spend countless hours chasing marginal improvements—researching funds, tweaking allocations, timing entries and exits—yet hesitate to spend a single focused hour building a long-term system that would eliminate the need for most of that labour. That one hour, if approached with clarity and commitment, can outperform years of anxiety, hesitation, and false starts. The difference lies not in complexity, but in intentionality. When properly designed, a well-aligned robo-advisor setup can become a silent engine of compounding wealth—not because it demands your constant attention, but because it earns your trust.

The central promise of robo-advisors is not automation for automation's sake. It is architecture. They allow investors to design a system once and let it work continuously, quietly, and intelligently over decades. That's not a technological convenience—it's a philosophical pivot. It replaces intermittent control with enduring structure. But it requires a front-loaded hour of thoughtful configuration. Done poorly, the setup process is perfunctory: name, income, risk slider, click "agree." Done well, it's a strategic act of self-understanding that rivals any financial planning meeting in depth and durability.

Let's be specific. What does a serious, high-integrity onboarding process look like? And how can it yield generational outcomes in under sixty minutes?

The first and most underrated step is *emotional clarity.* Before you input a single figure, you must ask what this system is for—not in generic terms, but in lived terms. Are you seeking freedom from salary dependence by age 50? Are you preparing for your child's education in ten years? Do you want to shift to part-time work in a decade and need supplemental income? Each answer reshapes time horizon, asset allocation, and contribution strategy. Without this clarity, even the best algorithm will optimise for the wrong outcome.

Once intent is sharpened, the next move is *platform selection.* While most robo-advisors offer similar technical features—automated rebalancing, tax-loss harvesting, ETF-based portfolios—they differ meaningfully in tone, transparency, and underlying philosophy. A minimalist platform like Vanguard may appeal to those who value restraint and institutional credibility. Wealthfront, by contrast, attracts users seeking advanced features like 529 planning and Smart Beta tilts. Nutmeg offers a UK-specific interface with visual clarity and socially responsible investment options. Betterment leads with user experience and goal-based tracking, while Scripbox in India integrates household-level planning with regional financial context. The point isn't to pick the "best" platform, but the one that *mirrors your values and temperament.* You are outsourcing execution—not judgment. Alignment matters.

With the platform chosen, you now engage the decision that most investors rush through: *risk profiling.* Most systems will ask a version of the same questions: "How would you feel if your portfolio dropped 20%?" "What's your investment horizon?" "How much volatility can you stomach?" The danger lies in answering aspirationally rather than truthfully. People report the investor they wish they were, not the one they are. But markets punish fiction. If you've never experienced a downturn, consider this: how did you feel during the COVID crash? Did you check your accounts obsessively? Did you panic-sell? Did you freeze? These are the emotional fingerprints that should inform your risk profile—not abstract ideas about courage. Be honest. Conservative is not a flaw. Aggressive is not a virtue. The right allocation is the one you can hold *through real fear.*

After risk is calibrated, you proceed to *funding and contribution automation.* This is where the compounding engine is actually built. Set up automatic transfers aligned with your income cycle. Even £200 per month, auto-debited and invisibly invested, becomes transformational over time. But this step is often skipped or delayed. Many users tinker endlessly with the interface—changing allocations, adjusting forecasts—but never connect their bank. Without automation, there is no system—only wishful thinking.

Here's a moment where the one-hour thesis becomes real. Assume you set up a £500 monthly contribution to a globally diversified 80/20 stock-bond portfolio, with automatic rebalancing and reinvested dividends. Historical data suggests such a strategy, over 25 years, could compound to over £350,000—depending on market performance and fees. That outcome is not based on genius. It's based on *non-intervention.* You didn't stock-pick. You didn't time the market. You didn't panic in downturns. You built a system—and then respected it.

Once the technical components are configured, there's one final layer: *periodic review cadence.* Not constant tinkering—*cadence.* Set a calendar reminder: one hour, once per year. In that hour, revisit your life—not your portfolio. Has your income changed? Have your goals shifted? Has your risk capacity increased or decreased due to life events? Then and only then, adjust the system. Outside of that hour, your job is not to monitor. It's to live. This redefines the investor's role—not as a controller, but as a steward.

Many of the wealthiest, most grounded investors follow this model. They don't wake up at 6 a.m. to track earnings reports or refresh stock tickers. They set up intentional systems that are allowed to breathe. They know that wealth is not built through micro-decisions, but through disciplined inaction. *One hour of serious thinking can outperform years of shallow hustle.*

For those still sceptical, consider the counterfactual. What does a lack of system produce? Fragmented accounts. Random purchases. Emotional allocation. Forgotten holdings. Tax inefficiency. And above all, decision fatigue. The mind burns energy trying to compensate for structural absence. The hour you don't spend upfront becomes 100 hours of reactive maintenance. That's not just inefficient. It's psychologically corrosive.

There's also a deeper philosophical shift at stake. When you commit to a system, you are saying something radical in a culture obsessed with novelty: *I trust compounding more than control.* That's not passivity. That's conviction. You are choosing structure over spectacle. Simplicity over stimulation. Long-term logic over short-term noise.

Let's recap this in human terms. What happens during this decisive hour?

1. You clarify your emotional and financial intent.

2. You choose a platform whose philosophy matches yours.

3. You answer the risk questions with humility, not bravado.

4. You automate your contributions with commitment.

5. You schedule an annual review—not for control, but for coherence.

This is not financial minimalism for its own sake. This is architectural thinking. You are designing an environment where your best financial instincts can thrive—and your worst ones are gently bypassed.

Every investor believes they'll act rationally in the future. Very few do. That's why systems matter. That's why the hour matters. It's not just about returns. It's about identity. You are choosing to become a person who builds wealth by alignment, not by obsession. That choice is made, not in markets, but in moments—like this hour.

One hour of intentional design can replace a decade of financial anxiety. But only if it's treated with the seriousness it deserves. Not as a setup. As a statement. And once made, that statement echoes—quietly, powerfully—for decades.

# Chapter 5
# Rebalancing Without Obsessing

There exists a tacit assumption in investing that goes largely unquestioned: the more frequently you engage with your portfolio, the more control you possess. For those drawn to analysis and meticulousness, the notion is alluring. Yet research from decades of behavioural finance paints a starkly different picture. The gravest threat to long-term wealth is seldom market gyrations, geopolitical upheaval, or inflation. It is, in fact, you—your impulses, your reactions to headlines, losses, and moments of overconfidence. And nowhere is this danger more pronounced than in the seemingly innocuous act of rebalancing.

This chapter seeks to recalibrate that instinct. Not by urging disengagement, but by presenting a superior alternative: intelligent, principled restraint. We will examine why algorithmic rebalancing frequently surpasses human attempts, not only in raw returns but in behavioural sustainability. We will unpack the subtle mechanisms—tax-loss harvesting, deferred gains—that quietly compound advantage. Most importantly, we will outline a minimalist review habit that honours your values while eliminating constant vigilance. Rebalancing, after all, should be a system, not a source of stress.

At its essence, rebalancing is the act of returning a portfolio to its target allocation. If equities surge while bonds lag, your portfolio drifts toward unintended risk. Rebalancing trims the outperformers and augments the underperformers, restoring equilibrium. This is discipline, not optimisation. Left unchecked, a portfolio slowly mutates into a different entity—often more volatile and misaligned with your intentions.

But human intervention complicates the picture. Investors delay, overact, or allow emotion to dictate timing. Fear, greed, or the latest headline often masquerade as prudence. "I'll wait until the next rate change." "Tech is due for a correction; I'll hold off." Mechanical processes become psychological battlegrounds. Here, algorithms excel.

Modern robo-advisors implement either threshold-based or time-based rebalancing. Threshold systems act when allocations drift beyond predefined limits, say ±5%. Time-based approaches run quarterly, semi-annually, or annually. Both eliminate emotional noise. No guessing, no obsession with market chatter—just steady, rule-bound adjustment. Over time, this consistency produces behavioural alpha: gains derived not from prediction, but from disciplined execution.

Consider Vanguard's research comparing annual, threshold, and non-rebalancing strategies over 25 years. Returns were broadly similar, yet rebalanced portfolios exhibited significantly lower volatility, translating into superior risk-adjusted performance. The differentiator was not foresight or luck—it was the absence of panic, a domain in which algorithms naturally excel.

Yet human judgement retains its place. Strategic intervention is warranted when life itself changes: a career shift, inheritance, business sale, or a child's education. Markets are not triggers; life events are. Recognising this distinction is crucial.

Algorithmic management also brings tax advantages once reserved for high-net-worth investors. Robo-advisors continuously scan portfolios, executing tax-loss harvesting by selling depreciated securities and replacing them with correlated alternatives. Exposure remains, losses are recorded for tax purposes, and gains deferred. These subtle, cumulative advantages quietly enhance net returns over decades—without any manual effort.

Still, many investors cannot resist compulsive checking. Not for lack of trust, but out of a fear of passivity. Here, a critical point must be drawn: strategic non-interference is not disengagement. Exercising restraint is an elevated form of control, but only if ritualised, or the temptation to meddle becomes irresistible.

A healthy review ritual is deliberate and infrequent: semi-annual, perhaps an hour-long. The focus is alignment, not reaction. Ask: does my portfolio still reflect my values? Have my goals or risk tolerance shifted due to age, experience, or income? If the answer is no, resist the impulse to adjust. Integrity, not change, is the aim. Done consistently, this is not inertia—it is design.

Compare this with typical investor behaviour. DALBAR studies show the average retail investor underperforms the market by more than 4% annually, largely due to mistimed trades. Buying high, selling low, and over-trading are common errors. The gap between market potential and realised returns is not intelligence—it is emotional discipline. Often, the most effective investors are those least involved, protected from their own instincts by systems they've built.

Rebalancing is therefore not a mere tactical exercise; it is a test of philosophy. Do you privilege systems over stories, process over prediction, alignment over action? The rebalancing approach you adopt mirrors your overall investment mindset. It is the humility to allow machines to act where your instincts might overreach, the maturity to permit automation to safeguard your wealth from your own impulses.

This chapter explores rebalancing technically, behaviourally, and philosophically. You will learn the mechanisms, understand where human input enhances or corrodes outcomes, and appreciate the long-term significance of tax efficiency. You will also establish a minimalist, repeatable review ritual—anchoring your portfolio to values rather than anxiety.

Daily portfolio checks are unnecessary. Trust the architecture you've built and approach reviews with respect, not obsession. Performance emerges not from constant intervention, but from disciplined maintenance over time. In the decades-long horizon of investing, discipline—not fleeting insight—is what truly builds wealth. This chapter shows how to preserve it, with precision, intention, and the right measure of distance.

## How Algorithms Stay Rational When You Don't

The markets reward discipline, not drama. And yet, most individual investors behave like amateur pilots in turbulent skies—gripping the controls tighter just when they should let the autopilot take over. Rebalancing, a foundational investing discipline, is meant to correct a portfolio's drift, nudging it back to its intended shape. But in human hands, even this mechanical task becomes a stage for improvisation, emotion, and unforced errors. What's needed is not more information, but better insulation—from ourselves. Algorithms provide precisely that. They don't guess, panic, or argue. They just execute. And over time, that consistency compounds into advantage.

The first thing to understand is that algorithmic rebalancing is not a flashy innovation. It is a quiet commitment to policy—executed perfectly. When a robo-advisor manages your portfolio, it begins by setting target allocations: say, 70% equities, 30% bonds. As markets shift, your portfolio drifts. Equities surge, and now they account for 75%. That's not inherently bad, but it introduces unintended risk. The portfolio is no longer aligned with your original tolerance. The algorithm trims equities and buys more bonds to restore balance. No ego. No debate. Just calibration.

Contrast this with how most investors approach the same task. The moment they notice equities are up, a cascade of psychological distortions begins. Should I ride the momentum? What if I sell and miss more upside? Maybe I should wait for a pullback. These are not decisions; they are justifications for inaction—or worse, for overreaction. Behavioural finance has documented these patterns for decades. *Overconfidence bias*, where people overestimate their ability to predict outcomes. *Recency bias*, where recent performance is mistaken for enduring trend. *Loss aversion*, which makes selling a winning asset feel like self-sabotage. Humans know rebalancing is good for them. They just can't do it reliably.

One of the clearest demonstrations of this comes from the annual "Behaviour Gap" research conducted by DALBAR, which tracks the difference between market returns and investor returns. Over a 20-year period, the S&P 500 returned roughly 8–9% annually. The average investor captured only around 4–5%. The culprit? Timing errors—buying high, selling low, and endlessly second-guessing.

Algorithms don't outperform because they're smarter. *They outperform because they're obedient.*

Rebalancing algorithms operate like self-correcting autopilots. Imagine a commercial jet en route from London to Singapore. It doesn't fly in a perfect straight line. It veers slightly off course thousands of times. But the autopilot makes micro-adjustments—quietly, constantly, and without ceremony. The plane still arrives precisely on schedule. Now imagine if the pilot disabled autopilot every ten minutes to "manually optimise" the route based on gut feeling. You'd never land, or worse—you'd crash. That's what most investors do. They replace policy with instinct. Algorithms, mercifully, do not.

This doesn't mean human input is irrelevant. It means it belongs at a higher altitude—*before* the flight begins. Your job is to set the right destination, map out your risk preferences, and choose the vehicle. Once that's done, meddling with the controls mid-flight is more likely to cause harm than help. Algorithmic rebalancing doesn't suppress your freedom. It protects the integrity of your decisions when your psychology is least reliable.

It also introduces efficiencies that most investors are simply not trained to exploit. Take *threshold-based rebalancing*, one of the more nuanced strategies used by robo-advisors like Wealthfront and Betterment. Instead of rebalancing on a fixed schedule (say, quarterly), the system monitors your allocations daily and only rebalances when an asset class deviates beyond a defined boundary—say, 5% from its target. This reduces unnecessary transactions, optimises for tax efficiency, and ensures the portfolio only intervenes when it *matters*. Humans are terrible at enforcing such rules consistently. Even institutional managers struggle. Algorithms don't.

The benefits aren't just mathematical. They are deeply behavioural. By delegating rebalancing, investors reduce the urge to constantly monitor and tinker. This separation creates emotional distance—

what psychologists call "decision space." The fewer choices you must make under stress, the fewer mistakes you're likely to make. Automation is not abdication. *It's preemptive wisdom.*

To illustrate, consider two investors: Marcus and Priya. Marcus checks his portfolio weekly, reads economic forecasts obsessively, and attempts to rebalance manually based on his interpretations of market cycles. In 2020, spooked by early pandemic losses, he sold half his equity positions, planning to "buy back in when things settled." They never did. He re-entered the market in late 2021—after missing most of the recovery. Priya, by contrast, set up her portfolio with a robo-advisor in 2017. She defined her risk profile, agreed on allocation rules, and hasn't made a single discretionary change since. Her account rebalanced automatically during the downturn, harvesting losses and restoring alignment. Her portfolio performed better—not because she knew more, but because she *interfered less.*

Of course, no algorithm is perfect. There are legitimate critiques around over-rebalancing, short-termism, and the nuances of illiquid asset classes. But these are marginal concerns. For the vast majority of investors, the risks of doing too little pale in comparison to the risks of doing too much. The greater danger is not omission—it is compulsion. Rebalancing is a lever best operated by protocol, not impulse.

This raises a deeper philosophical point: investors don't just want returns. They want *narratives*—a sense that they are steering, acting, influencing outcomes. Delegating to algorithms can feel like surrender. But that discomfort reveals something profound. The point of rational investing is not to prove your intelligence. It's to *get out of your own way*. Machines don't remove human agency. They *refine* it. They enable investors to express their intent at the highest level—without succumbing to interference at the lowest.

We must also appreciate how rebalancing algorithms evolve. They aren't static spreadsheets. Many are now built atop machine learning models that optimise for tax implications, transaction costs, and risk tolerances in real time. For example, Wealthfront's "Stock-level Tax-Loss Harvesting" technology identifies opportunities to sell underperforming individual equities, not just ETFs—something nearly impossible to execute manually without professional-grade software. These aren't gimmicks. They are structural improvements in execution fidelity. And the investor who benefits is the one who trusts the process enough to let it work.

Even sceptics must contend with a simple truth: most people cannot out-time the market. And those who can, rarely do it consistently. The institutional data is damning. Active funds underperform benchmarks with stubborn regularity. The real arbitrage today is not intellectual, but *behavioural.* Automation secures that edge—not through foresight, but through restraint.

Ultimately, rebalancing is a test of temperament. Are you willing to build a portfolio governed by principle rather than performance? Can you let systems correct your drift instead of indulging every reactive impulse? These are not technical questions. They are psychological thresholds. And algorithms, far from stripping investors of control, invite them to embrace a deeper version of it—the kind that resists the illusion of mastery, and settles instead for mastery of self.

You do not need to watch every market move to win. You need a system that reacts less than you would. The best portfolios are not those with the most clever trades, but those least exposed to human error. Automation isn't a shortcut. It's a structure. One that, if you let it, can hold the line when your instincts would not.

## When to Intervene—and When to Walk Away

A well-designed investment system does not demand your constant presence. In fact, the highest form of portfolio sophistication is not endless optimisation, but *disciplined restraint.* Modern investors often conflate involvement with intelligence, action with control. But the true wisdom lies in knowing when intervention adds value—and when it merely adds noise. The most successful long-term investors are not those who monitor markets obsessively, but those who intervene sparingly, with purpose. Knowing the difference is not a matter of strategy—it is a matter of self-awareness.

To begin, it's critical to distinguish between *structural adjustments* and *emotional intrusions*. Structural adjustments respond to tangible life events: a major salary increase, the birth of a child, a relocation to another country, or a shift in retirement horizon. These moments legitimately change your financial architecture. They are not fluctuations in feeling—they are revisions in fact. Emotional intrusions, by contrast, are impulsive. They are triggered by market headlines, peer conversations, social media panic, or a portfolio drop of 7% in a single week. One is a recalibration of purpose; the other is a reaction to discomfort.

Let's start with the few instances when stepping in makes clear rational sense. A sudden increase in income—say, a new job or promotion—offers an opportunity to increase contributions or expand risk capacity. If you were previously limited to a 60/40 equity-bond split because of a tight cash buffer, a higher income may justify a move to 70/30 or even 80/20, provided your risk tolerance supports it. Likewise, a sharp decrease in income or job loss calls for immediate adjustment: either to reduce risk, draw down cash buffers, or pause contributions. These are not hypothetical shifts. They are concrete facts that affect your investment horizon and cash flow management.

Another critical intervention point is life-stage change. The arrival of a child, for instance, might prompt you to start a junior ISA, a 529 plan, or some other educational savings vehicle. A divorce may change your legal and tax considerations. A geographic move may open or close access to certain account types or investment products. These are not interruptions to a set-it-and-forget-it model;

they are its essential recalibrations. Automation is powerful, but it is not clairvoyant. It needs you to supply the context.

But here's the paradox: the vast majority of events investors treat as intervention-worthy are not. The Dow dropping 800 points. The pound weakening against the dollar. A friend bragging about a new crypto allocation. None of these warrant action. They only feel urgent because they threaten our sense of stability or status. And the problem with acting on emotional stimuli is not just that the timing is wrong—it's that the rationale is unstable. If you move into cash because markets feel scary, what data point tells you when to get back in? What signal do you trust? These decisions don't live in spreadsheets. They live in moods. And moods are no place to manage capital.

Consider the 2008 financial crisis. Many investors sold near the bottom, convinced they were escaping deeper pain. Most did not return to equities until years later—if at all—missing the substantial gains that followed. They intervened because the market's behaviour made them anxious. But anxiety is not an investing variable. It's a psychological response. Automated systems, on the other hand, rebalanced portfolios during the crisis—buying more equities when they were cheap, restoring allocation discipline. The intervention they made was mathematical, not emotional. And over time, it paid.

This raises an uncomfortable truth: one of the hardest parts of intelligent investing is learning to *walk away*—not in surrender, but in discipline. The instinct to do something must be re-trained. Most portfolios don't fail because of the market. They fail because of the investor. The problem isn't insufficient involvement—it's misdirected involvement. Instead of refining the plan, we try to outperform it. We confuse presence with prudence. But *the real sophistication lies in building a system robust enough that you don't need to supervise it constantly.*

This is where a minimalist framework for review becomes essential. Rather than checking your portfolio every few days—a habit correlated with reduced investment satisfaction and increased reactive behaviour—establish a ritual. Once or twice a year, conduct a structured review. Ask four questions: Has my income materially changed? Have my long-term goals shifted? Have my liquidity needs increased or decreased? Has my risk tolerance been altered by new life circumstances—not just by market performance? If the answer to all four is no, the correct course is almost always: *leave it alone.*

These review rituals are not about tinkering. They are about reaffirming alignment. Do my investments still reflect the life I'm building? Has anything about my external reality changed enough to warrant a response? If not, then resist the urge to optimise. Many investors confuse motion with progress. But portfolios, like gardens, don't grow faster because you dig them up every week.

To further illustrate, consider a case study: Elena, a 41-year-old professional based in Edinburgh, began investing through a robo-advisor in 2016. She had a medium-aggressive risk profile and contributed monthly to a general investment account and ISA. In March 2020, when markets plunged, she received a flurry of emails from colleagues talking about "going to cash." She logged in, saw her account down 17%, and closed the browser. She stuck to her annual review schedule, which was due that June. By then, the portfolio had largely recovered. No changes were necessary. Her only "action" was inaction, informed by structure.

Elena's restraint wasn't apathy. It was design. Her system was calibrated to absorb volatility without summoning her for every shock. That structure is the point. Investing is not about reacting to every fluctuation. It's about aligning capital with goals and trusting the process that links them.

Of course, there are exceptions—rare but critical. A sudden windfall, such as an inheritance or business sale, may require one-off portfolio adjustments to reallocate for risk balance or tax efficiency. Terminal illness or unexpected disability may necessitate a shift to income-generating investments or cash preservation. These are not "market events." They are *life events*. And life events, not market noise, are the only valid triggers for portfolio reassessment.

This distinction between signal and noise, intervention and interference, is not intuitive. It must be taught—and practised. Most people, especially high performers in other domains, are conditioned to equate effort with outcomes. But the capital markets don't reward intensity. They reward coherence. The investor who intervenes only when life changes—not when markets wobble—is not disengaged. They are *disciplined*. They understand that clarity is rare, and when you have it, your job is to protect it—not complicate it.

If you must act, act structurally. Update your goals. Adjust your contribution levels. Reassess your time horizon. But do not micromanage. A portfolio is not a pet project. It's a machine. Its primary job is not to impress you—it's to work when you're not watching.

Ultimately, what's at stake here is not just financial return, but *psychological freedom*. The less reactive your investing life becomes, the more bandwidth you reclaim for everything else that matters. The aim is not to eliminate agency. It's to elevate it. By learning when to intervene and when to walk away, you transform from a stressed-out speculator to a rational architect. You stop confusing market movement with personal meaning. And you begin to experience the deep, quiet confidence of a plan that works *without your constant input*. That's not detachment. That's mastery.

## Tax Efficiency: Invisible Wins That Compound

One of the quietest truths in wealth building is this: the difference between good and great investors often isn't who made the highest returns, but who *kept more of what they made*. The allure of market-beating strategies or exotic asset classes often blinds investors to the quieter, compounding force sitting in plain sight—tax efficiency. While risk, return, and time horizon dominate the conversation, it's taxes that quietly siphon away value year after year. And it's automation—not bravado—that is increasingly proving to be the superior defence.

When investors think of growth, they tend to think in headlines—big wins, double-digit returns, a well-timed market call. But those narratives rarely factor in what happens *after* the returns are made. Capital gains, dividend taxes, transaction fees, poorly timed withdrawals—all eat into what appears on paper. The illusion is one of control: that returns alone determine wealth. In truth, *frictionless compounding is a tax-sensitive affair.* Every percentage point lost to inefficiency is a percentage point that never compounds.

This is where automated systems—especially modern robo-advisors—demonstrate a structural advantage. Their strength is not just in diversification or low fees. It's in their capacity to apply complex, nuanced tax strategies with robotic consistency and without behavioural interference. One of the most powerful, yet underappreciated, examples of this is *tax-loss harvesting.*

At its core, tax-loss harvesting is the process of selling investments that have declined in value to realise a capital loss, then reinvesting the proceeds in a similar, but not identical, asset to maintain exposure. The realised loss offsets other gains in the portfolio, reducing taxable income and deferring tax liability. For the investor, this appears almost invisible. But over time, it adds up in ways that few manual investors can replicate.

To appreciate its real impact, consider a scenario involving two investors: Daniel and Priya. Both invest £50,000 in a diversified equity portfolio. Daniel uses a traditional DIY brokerage account. Priya uses a robo-advisor with automated tax-loss harvesting enabled. After a volatile year, markets rebound, but along the way there were short-term downturns. Priya's platform sold certain ETFs during those dips and replaced them with near substitutes—capturing £3,000 in losses while maintaining her market exposure. These losses offset gains elsewhere in her account, reducing her capital gains tax for the year by £600. That £600 stays invested.

Compounded over 20 years at 6%, it quietly grows to over £1,900. And that's from one year's worth of harvesting. Repeat the process consistently, and it becomes a compounding engine of its own.

The key here is not just the mechanism—it's the *consistency*. Most human investors either forget to harvest, miss the ideal windows, or are paralysed by decision fatigue. Robo-advisors, by contrast, can scan for harvesting opportunities daily, sometimes even multiple times a day, without blinking. This constant vigilance is not emotional. It's computational. It doesn't care whether markets are "uncertain" or whether the investor feels optimistic. It just executes.

Of course, tax efficiency is not only about harvesting losses. It's also about *deferring gains*. This principle—postponing taxable events until later—aligns with the basic mechanics of compounding. The longer you delay paying taxes on gains, the more capital remains invested, generating additional returns. When investors prematurely rebalance or chase performance, they often trigger taxable events that erode their base. Automated platforms, especially those designed with tax-optimisation algorithms, can rebalance *within* tax-advantaged envelopes or harvest gains selectively, in ways designed to limit liability.

It's worth pausing to reflect on how human instincts often work against this discipline. When markets rise sharply, many investors are tempted to sell winners to "lock in profits." But this behaviour often triggers avoidable taxes. Conversely, when markets fall, they avoid selling losers—unwilling to "realise a loss" even when it offers a tangible tax benefit. The irony is stark: we avoid losses when we should harvest them and lock in gains when we should defer them. In both cases, *emotion becomes a tax*. Automation, by contrast, is indifferent. It makes the optimal move even when it doesn't feel satisfying.

Nowhere is this more visible than in the realm of asset location. The principle is straightforward: place tax-inefficient investments (like bonds or REITs) in tax-advantaged accounts (such as ISAs or SIPPs) and keep tax-efficient assets (like equities with low turnover) in taxable accounts. In practice, very few DIY investors implement this correctly. Robo-advisors, however, often manage portfolios across account types with asset location algorithms that automatically optimise where assets are held. The result is an architecture that supports long-term compounding without drawing unnecessary attention from the tax authorities.

Critics might argue that tax efficiency is only marginal—that it's a "nice to have" rather than a core driver of returns. But this misunderstands the cumulative nature of drag. A 1% higher after-tax return compounded over 30 years is not a rounding error—it's the difference between financial adequacy and abundance. And it's achieved not through outsmarting markets, but by avoiding unforced errors.

More provocatively, tax efficiency exposes a deeper tension in personal finance: the bias toward visible wins. We are wired to celebrate overt victories—beating a benchmark, identifying a hot stock, timing the market. But tax efficiency is a *quiet win.* It doesn't shout. It doesn't trend on social media. It doesn't deliver adrenaline. It just compounds. Year after year. Invisibly. That's precisely what makes it so powerful—and why automation is often its only reliable steward.

Even among professional wealth managers, the consistent application of tax strategies is often uneven. An adviser may discuss tax-loss harvesting in theory, but they aren't monitoring a client's portfolio every day to execute it systematically. Nor are they rebalancing across multiple accounts in real time based on asset location rules. These are tasks uniquely suited to algorithmic oversight. Not because humans are incapable—but because humans are distracted, busy, emotional, and fallible. *Automation doesn't forget.* And in the realm of tax efficiency, memory and timing are everything.

To be clear, not all robo platforms offer the same degree of tax optimisation. Betterment, for example, has long positioned itself as a leader in this space, with sophisticated tax-coordinated portfolios and daily harvesting scans. Wealthfront uses a similar approach and includes features like Stock-Level Tax-Loss Harvesting, which further enhances customisation. Vanguard's Personal Advisor Services, while more traditional, have integrated tax-aware rebalancing into their hybrid models. In the UK, platforms like Nutmeg and Moneyfarm offer varying degrees of tax optimisation within the ISA and pension framework. But the unifying thread is this: where automation is allowed to act without interruption, *tax drag can be consistently minimised.*

None of this absolves the investor of responsibility. Tax rules change. Personal circumstances evolve. At higher income brackets or with multiple jurisdictions involved, bespoke advice may still be warranted. But at the foundational level—the level where most investors operate—automated tax efficiency is not a gimmick. It is *strategy embedded in structure.*

The best part? It doesn't require constant attention. Once enabled, tax-loss harvesting, deferred gain strategies, and asset location protocols continue to function while you do anything else with your life. They generate no dopamine, no thrill. But they quietly ensure that more of your return remains yours. Not once. Every year.

And over decades, that's not a feature. That's a revolution hiding in the background.

## Rituals Over Reactions: Designing a Review Habit

Most people check their portfolios the way they check social media: impulsively, irrationally, and usually in reaction to something external. A news headline. A market drop. A coworker's hot tip. And then they respond—not with strategy, but with fear, envy, or overconfidence. It's not because they lack intelligence; it's because they lack *structure.* If left ungoverned, our psychology drifts toward drama. Markets offer an endless theatre for this tendency. But for those serious about long-term wealth, *discipline beats drama every time.*

Designing a portfolio review ritual is about reclaiming control—not from the markets, but from ourselves. It begins with recognising that frequent checking does not equal diligence. In fact, it's often the opposite. Obsessive monitoring magnifies volatility and distorts our perception of risk. A 20% decline viewed daily feels catastrophic; viewed annually, it's often just noise. This is not a call for ignorance, but for *intentional awareness*. The investor who reviews their portfolio once or twice a year, with clarity and composure, is often more informed than the one checking it five times a day in a state of nervous agitation.

A well-structured review ritual serves a deeper function than performance tracking. It becomes a values-alignment tool. A moment to ask not "Did I beat the market?" but "Is my strategy still serving the life I want?" Without that anchoring question, all numbers are unmoored. They seduce us into optimisation without reflection—risking our sanity in pursuit of someone else's definition of success.

So what does a minimalist yet meaningful review ritual actually look like?

Start by *anchoring the review to a specific time.* Twice a year is sufficient—ideally once in January to calibrate goals and once in July as a mid-year check. These should be scheduled events, not emotional reactions. Set a calendar reminder. Make it non-negotiable. The power lies not in the frequency but in the rhythm. Like a physical exam or a dental visit, its value is preventive, not reactive.

Next, *frame the review with three simple questions*:

1. Has anything changed in my life circumstances or financial goals that requires a portfolio adjustment?

2. Does my current asset allocation still reflect my true risk tolerance and time horizon?

3. Am I acting on long-term principles, or short-term emotions?

These questions do more than collect data; they interrogate *alignment.* They invite the investor to review not just the portfolio, but the mindset driving it. This is where ritual becomes reflection.

Consider a real-world example: someone in their early 40s, planning to retire at 60. In January, they review their portfolio and notice a strong overweight in tech stocks due to recent outperformance. Rather than react with excitement or greed, they revisit their original allocation—designed to balance growth with risk mitigation—and initiate a simple rebalance. No market timing. No prediction. Just a return to strategic equilibrium. In July, they check again. No major life changes, no dramatic portfolio shifts, but they use the review to reaffirm their strategy and resist the temptation to chase trends. This is *process over performance.* It looks boring. But it's how wealth endures.

Contrast that with the typical pattern: an investor sees a sharp drop, logs in, panics, sells low, and buys something that just rose. Or hears a friend made 40% in crypto, checks their own performance, and suddenly feels behind—despite having met every goal they set for the year. *Comparison is a corrosive benchmark.* Without a ritualised frame of reference, even strong returns can feel inadequate.

It's important to remember that the function of reviewing your portfolio is not to *tweak*, it's to *tune*. The temptation to make changes every time you log in is strong. But most wealth is not lost through poor strategy—it's lost through *overactivity*. The review ritual should include a deliberate pause. A forced reflection period, even if just 48 hours, before implementing any changes. This friction protects you from yourself. Automation handles rebalancing. Algorithms manage drift. Your job is simply to ensure the machine is pointed in the right direction—and to leave it alone when it is.

There is also a psychological edge to this design. When reviews are structured and sparse, *they feel more meaningful.* You engage deeply. You think systemically. You take notes. Some investors even write a brief "portfolio letter to self," outlining their reasoning, adjustments, and reaffirmed principles. Over time, this creates a rich audit trail—not of returns, but of reasoning. You begin to see your growth not just in net worth, but in clarity.

What's especially powerful is that this ritual decouples your attention from *volatility.* Markets will always be volatile. But if you only look periodically, volatility loses its grip on your psyche. You stop reacting to every wiggle in the line. You build emotional immunity. And that stability of attention is what gives long-term strategies the room to compound.

For investors using robo-advisors, this ritual complements automation perfectly. You don't need to check whether your portfolio has rebalanced—it already has. You don't need to manually harvest tax losses—they've been captured algorithmically. What you *do* need to check is whether your goals have changed, whether your risk tolerance still holds, and whether you're psychologically committed to your strategy. The ritual becomes less about numbers and more about *narrative.*

This shift—from reaction to ritual, from metrics to meaning—is subtle but profound. It echoes a broader movement in modern finance: away from performance-chasing, and toward *purpose-driven investing.* When you know what your money is for, you no longer need to obsess over every movement. You are free to focus on life itself—secure in the knowledge that your financial system is quietly doing its job.

Let's be clear: the investor who reviews their portfolio quarterly or even monthly is not inherently wrong. But unless those reviews are part of a well-designed, emotionally grounded process, they can quickly devolve into *ritualised anxiety.* The minimalist approach forces discipline. It limits the bandwidth for impulsivity and creates space for more intentional decision-making.

Rituals also age well. A 30-year-old checking their portfolio every week may find it thrilling. A 55-year-old juggling family, health, and legacy planning often wants *clarity, not constant noise.* A ritualised approach scales with life. It matures with you. And perhaps most importantly, it cultivates a form of *investor self-trust*—the confidence that your system works, your goals are valid, and your attention can be spent on things more meaningful than the market's latest mood swing.

In this way, a minimalist portfolio review isn't just a tactic. It's a philosophy. A rejection of reactive finance culture. A quiet vote for intentional living. A space to remember that your portfolio is not your personality, and its daily fluctuations are not your identity.

Twice a year. One hour. Three questions. A short letter to yourself. No drama. No panic. Just a moment to realign your strategy with your values. *Let the market move. Let the systems work. Let yourself live.*

# Chapter 6
# The Emotional Cost of DIY Investing

It starts innocuously. A colleague mentions a promising stock, a YouTube clip flashes with tales of market-beating returns, a sleek app makes trading feel instantaneous, effortless, even thrilling. Soon enough, your portfolio is open, notifications pinging with every tick, and each uptick in price delivers a tiny surge of satisfaction. But behind this glossy veneer of empowerment lurks something less enticing: fatigue. Not simply the exhaustion of monitoring markets, but the deeper, creeping toll of being perpetually responsible for something you barely comprehend—and pretending otherwise.

DIY investing markets a narrative of independence, yet it rarely accounts for its cognitive cost. The modern retail investor faces a cascade of choices, each presented as freedom but often functioning as decision fatigue in disguise. Daily, new stocks beckon for analysis, ETFs demand comparison, headlines clamor for interpretation, economic forecasts require conjecture. "Stay informed," we are told—subtly translating into "stay anxious." Research from the University of Minnesota demonstrates that frequent, even low-stakes financial decision-making erodes executive function over time, leaving people reactive rather than rational. The act of choosing, repeated incessantly, saps the very mental bandwidth required to make good choices.

This depletion is insidious. The trader who begins the morning scanning earnings reports may end the day compulsively refreshing Reddit threads. The investor who claims to "take control" of their finances finds sleep elusive during a market correction. Interviews with fatigued retail traders echo a common sentiment: "I thought I was being smart. I didn't realise I was just addicted." One 38-year-old tech worker likened his intense pandemic-era personal trading to "a second job I couldn't quit—even when it stopped making sense." DIY investing promises sovereignty, yet too often delivers cognitive entrapment.

Compounding the problem is the illusion of objectivity. Investors believe they make evidence-based decisions, when in reality they filter for confirmation. Confirmation bias, the human tendency to seek information that aligns with pre-existing beliefs, is amplified online. A crypto enthusiast spends hours reading bullish blogs while disregarding cautionary analysis—not out of irrationality, but because their mind selectively filters inputs threatening their narrative.

From this feedback loop emerges overconfidence: self-selected data reinforces beliefs, leading to riskier bets. Early successes cement misleading patterns. Anecdotes harden into personal folklore. "I always buy on Fridays," one trader joked. Another avoided companies after watching CEO interviews, trusting "gut feelings" about tone. Harmless individually, these habits often solidify into doctrine: untested, unquestioned, yet deeply believed. Experimentation calcifies into conviction.

The stakes extend beyond finances. Mental rigidity sets in. Investors optimise for stories rather than returns, dismissing data that conflicts with entrenched narratives. Even professional fund managers succumb to narrative coherence bias—believing stories that rationalise outcomes despite their predictive irrelevance. Retail investors, lacking systemic checks, face paralysis.

Underlying this behaviour is ego-protection. Changing strategy admits past error. Outsourcing to a system signals surrender of self-perceived superiority. DIY investors double down, not for effectiveness, but to safeguard identity. The market ceases to be a mechanism for wealth and becomes a mirror for self-worth. Delegation feels like defeat; surrender, a concession.

Yet the pivotal shift is evolutionary, not surrendering. Moving from ego-driven to evidence-based decision-making reframes the market as a system, not a contest. Performance-chasing yields to sustainability-focused design. Narratives are interrogated. Questions shift from "How smart am I?" to "What actually drives market behaviour?" The transformation is subtle but profound: trades decline, goals clarify, sleep improves.

This chapter maps that journey. It reveals how activity often masquerades as productivity, how early wins can trap you in unhelpful patterns, and how confidence rooted in data surpasses that founded on delusion. You will see why algorithms, for all their imperfections, frequently outperform well-intentioned human effort, and how biases—confirmation, hindsight—distort strategy. More importantly, it explores the emotional relief that comes from relinquishing perpetual control in favour of structured simplicity.

The cognitive cost of DIY investing is real. Each minute scanning tickers or second-guessing decisions drains mental bandwidth, diverting attention from career, relationships, health, and presence. While returns are measured in percentages, the psychic cost per point of alpha is rarely considered. This chapter brings that cost into focus.

This is not a critique of initiative. Learning, engaging, and understanding markets is commendable. Yet conflating involvement with mastery is a frequent pitfall. Markets reward discipline, not activity. Discipline often means doing less: letting systems operate where human impulse falters, attending to the architecture of a well-structured financial life rather than every individual trade.

DIY investing promises liberation. Without boundaries, it becomes bondage. The remedy is precision: knowing when to act, when to abstain, and how to design systems that compensate for human fallibility. This guidance is not about incapacity, complexity, or failure. It is about valuing time and attention, creating calm, sustainable, enduring strategies that serve life itself—not ego.

## Decision Fatigue Disguised as Empowerment

On the surface, DIY investing is framed as a modern triumph: technology has democratised finance, research tools are widely available, and platforms promise unprecedented control. With a few taps on a smartphone, anyone can become a "self-directed investor." It sounds empowering—and to a point, it is. But peel back the marketing language, and you uncover a quieter reality. What's sold as freedom is often just *unstructured responsibility*. What feels like progress is, in many cases, *cognitive overload with a shiny interface.* The supposed empowerment of constant decision-making in investing often leads not to better outcomes, but to psychological depletion.

Decision fatigue is a well-documented phenomenon in behavioural psychology. When faced with a series of choices—especially ones that require weighing trade-offs, tolerating ambiguity, or forecasting uncertain outcomes—our capacity to evaluate them rationally erodes over time. And unlike discrete decisions such as choosing what to eat for lunch, investing decisions come laced with perceived stakes, emotional attachment, and the ever-present illusion that "one wrong move could cost years of returns." The result is an environment where every choice *feels urgent*, but few are made from clarity.

The financial industry rarely acknowledges this, because decision-making sells. Platforms are built to maximise engagement. They send alerts, push updates, offer hot takes from "analysts" with questionable track records. Algorithms are trained to keep you watching. The more you interact, the more data they collect—and the more they encourage the illusion that being hyper-involved equals being intelligent. What's rarely discussed is the psychological cost: the erosion of focus, the paralysis of overchoice, the creeping anxiety that shadows each trade.

Take Arjun, a 33-year-old software engineer from Bangalore who started actively managing his investments during the 2020 lockdown. "I thought I'd be in and out of the markets in 20 minutes a day," he explained. "But it turned into hours. I had eight tabs open all the time—news, Twitter, charts, Reddit. I told myself I was being productive, but I wasn't making better decisions. I was just constantly doubting the last one." Arjun isn't alone. Interviews with retail investors across geographies reveal the same theme: the more decisions they felt responsible for, the less confident they became. And ironically, the more time they invested, the less satisfied they felt with their portfolios.

What makes this dynamic so insidious is that it mimics productivity. Investors convince themselves that staying busy—reading market commentary, adjusting asset allocations, reacting to news—is the sign of diligence. But in behavioural finance, this is recognised as *action bias*: the irrational preference for doing something over doing nothing, especially in uncertain conditions. In markets, where randomness often outweighs insight in the short term, this bias can be especially costly. You feel more engaged but are, in effect, chasing shadows.

Moreover, decision fatigue doesn't just impair the *quality* of choices; it alters the *criteria* by which those choices are made. Under cognitive load, individuals are more likely to default to heuristics—rules of thumb or gut instincts—rather than rigorous analysis. A 2018 study published in the Journal of Economic Behaviour & Organisation found that participants under mental strain made more impulsive trades, were more susceptible to framing effects, and had lower overall returns. In other words, the very mechanism that DIY investing demands—constant personal input—is precisely what degrades under pressure.

Another retail investor, Clara, a 41-year-old teacher from Bristol, shared her experience of managing a "diversified" portfolio of 24 ETFs. "At first, I thought I was being thorough," she admitted. "But it quickly became unmanageable. I was constantly rebalancing, reading up on emerging markets, trying to 'catch' sector rotations. I started waking up at 3 a.m. thinking about interest rate decisions in countries I didn't understand. It wasn't empowering—it was exhausting." Clara eventually automated her entire portfolio, not out of laziness, but out of necessity. "I realised my energy was finite. And it was being wasted on noise."

What Clara discovered is a truth few financial influencers promote: *autonomy is not the same as constant involvement.* A robust investing strategy doesn't require your attention every day. In fact, many of the world's most successful investors—from Warren Buffett to Jack

Bogle—emphasised *inactivity* as a virtue, not a vice. They understood that resilience often lies in designing systems that *resist* human interference, rather than depend on it. The irony is that automation, so often framed as a shortcut for the uninformed, is actually a form of *strategic restraint* for the informed.

This reframing is vital. Because at its core, decision fatigue in investing is not simply a cognitive issue—it's an *identity issue.* Many DIY investors conflate effort with intelligence, activity with mastery, and control with wisdom. When they're told to automate or simplify, they hear "surrender." But what if the deeper wisdom lies in *deciding less*, not more? What if success isn't found in squeezing alpha from every tick, but in aligning one's portfolio with one's life—and letting it run quietly in the background?

To make that shift requires an honest audit. Not of your portfolio, but of your temperament. Are you making choices out of strategy, or out of anxiety? Are your investment decisions driven by your goals, or by the digital architecture of the platform you're using? Are you reviewing your finances in a focused, intentional cadence—or constantly tweaking them in response to external noise?

One way to identify decision fatigue masquerading as empowerment is to track your emotional state around investing. If the dominant feelings are stress, compulsion, or doubt, something is misaligned. If you find yourself unable to unplug, rechecking market updates during dinner or comparing your returns against friends, it's a signal—not of engagement, but of cognitive strain. Empowered investors feel *calm.* They act with discipline. They understand that systems outperform willpower, especially in domains riddled with uncertainty and temptation.

The broader lesson is that the modern investing environment is not built to optimise your wellbeing—it's built to optimise your engagement. Every click, every refresh, every micro-decision serves someone else's business model. Escaping that treadmill is not laziness; it's clarity. You're not abdicating responsibility by deciding less. You're choosing to *spend your finite cognitive energy on decisions that actually matter*—career strategy, family planning, health, creative pursuits. Your portfolio is a means to support life, not an endless source of distraction within it.

There's dignity in automation. There's courage in simplicity. And there's profound intelligence in recognising that *being a good investor is not about how many decisions you make—it's about how few you need to make, because the important ones were already made well.* The next chapter builds on this insight. It explores how biases—confirmation, overconfidence, and storytelling—warp decision-making even further, and how evidence-based frameworks can liberate you from the self-imposed traps of DIY investing. But for now, the invitation is simple: put down the decision engine, step outside the volatility loop, and remember that stillness is not passivity. It's the discipline of the truly empowered.

## Confirmation Bias and the Echo Chamber of Overconfidence

Ask a room of self-directed investors whether they think they are more rational than the average participant in the market, and the majority will say yes. This is not hubris in the traditional sense—it's a cognitive blind spot that afflicts even the most numerate minds. DIY investing, with its promise of control and insight, has quietly become a breeding ground for one of behavioural finance's most pervasive distortions: *confirmation bias*. The tendency to seek, interpret, and remember information that confirms our existing beliefs is not just a psychological quirk—it's an invisible hand that steers investment decisions into narrower lanes, reinforcing overconfidence while quietly eroding portfolio resilience.

Most investors don't believe they're biased. They believe they're well-informed. They read reports, follow analysts, monitor charts. But a deeper inspection reveals that much of this "research" is merely *justification in disguise*. If an investor already suspects that tech stocks are undervalued, they will scan headlines for supportive narratives, dismissing bearish analyses as pessimistic noise or backward-looking speculation. The data may be factual, but the filter is emotional. And unlike in laboratory experiments, where biases can be controlled for, the investing world is rich with ambiguity—leaving ample room for selective interpretation to masquerade as due diligence.

The rise of online investing communities has exacerbated this tendency. Forums, subreddits, and social trading platforms offer an illusion of diversified opinion but often function as echo chambers. Algorithms are designed to show users what they're likely to agree with—curating a feed that flatters their instincts rather than challenges them. If you've ever watched a retail investor post a bullish thesis on a forum, you'll notice the replies tend to reinforce the narrative: "Good call." "Holding the same." "This one's going to the moon." Dissent is rare, and when it does appear, it's often drowned out or discredited as "FUD" (fear, uncertainty, and doubt). The result? *An ecosystem that rewards conviction over caution, and confidence over accuracy.*

This behavioural loop leads not only to flawed decisions but to distorted diversification. Investors convinced of a particular thesis—whether it's the inevitability of clean energy, the superiority of a favourite ETF, or the collapse of fiat currency—will over-allocate to reflect that belief. They may claim to be diversified, but in practice, they are making directional bets wrapped in the veneer of discipline. Asset classes become narratives. Risk becomes rhetoric. The illusion of control becomes self-reinforcing.

Consider the case of Dinesh, a 29-year-old data analyst from Mumbai who began investing in late 2020. Initially cautious, he found early success with small-cap tech stocks, fuelled in part by Twitter threads that validated his optimism. "The more I read, the more I believed I was ahead of the curve," he said. "I built spreadsheets, watched earnings calls, followed fund managers who echoed my thinking." But when the market corrected in early 2022, his portfolio fell sharply. He hadn't diversified—not because he didn't know how, but because every piece of "research" he consumed told him not to. "I thought I was being thorough. I was actually building a bubble around my own opinions."

Dinesh's experience is not exceptional. Studies show that overconfident investors trade more frequently, hold fewer assets, and underperform the market—especially after periods of success. A 2001 paper by Barber and Odean titled "Boys Will Be Boys: Gender, Overconfidence, and Common Stock Investment" found that men, who tend to be more overconfident in financial matters, traded 45% more than women and achieved lower net returns. Crucially, their trades weren't irrational—they were overconfidently rational. They *sought data to support their moves*, acted decisively, and ignored contradictory signals. Confirmation bias made their decisions feel well-grounded, when in reality, they were selectively informed.

This bias doesn't just affect individuals. Entire sectors have risen and fallen on the back of confirmation-fuelled investing. The cryptocurrency boom of 2020–2021 is a striking example. Investors created intricate belief systems around decentralisation, inflation hedging, and institutional adoption. They consumed content that supported these views—often from influencers with vested interests—and dismissed regulatory warnings or critiques as part of a conspiracy by the "old guard." It's not that crypto had no merit; it's that the surrounding discourse was so lopsided that any attempt at balanced analysis became socially penalised. When the correction came, many were left holding assets they no longer understood, in portfolios that had no defensive ballast.

Part of what makes confirmation bias so powerful is its comfort. Uncertainty is emotionally taxing. Contradiction is uncomfortable. In investing, where the stakes feel personal, the desire to find patterns that validate one's worldview is intense. And unlike in science, where hypotheses are meant to be tested against data, investing often reverses the process: the data is scanned for evidence to uphold the hypothesis. This inversion is subtle but critical. It creates a feedback loop in which confidence increases *even as objectivity declines*.

The antidote to confirmation bias is not to become a cynic or a contrarian for its own sake. It's to build *systematic mechanisms of dissent* into one's process. For institutional investors, this might mean red-team reviews or independent risk committees. For individuals, it can be as simple as forcing oneself to read the bear case for every thesis, or tracking how often your predictions actually play out. Ask: What would it take for me to be wrong? When would I exit this position? Have I heard a compelling argument *against* my view in the last month? If the answer to that last question is no, you're likely not investing—you're affirming. And affirming is not a strategy. It's a bias.

Diversification is not just about asset classes; it's about thought processes. A truly diversified investor doesn't just own a mix of equities, bonds, and alternatives—they consult different sources, weigh contradictory views, and remain humble in the face of uncertainty. This intellectual humility is increasingly rare in a world that rewards hot takes and punishes ambiguity. But it is, paradoxically, the foundation of durable confidence—the kind that allows an investor to hold through downturns not because they *know* they're right, but because they've built a portfolio that doesn't require them to be.

Overconfidence, like leverage, is seductive because it magnifies gains. But it also magnifies exposure to unseen risks—especially when those risks are embedded in one's own blind spots. The goal is not to eliminate conviction but to *temper it with reflection*. Not to abandon hypotheses but to expose them to disconfirmation. Not to stop believing in ideas but to interrogate the beliefs beneath them.

Investing is not a test of willpower or IQ. It is, more often, a test of *epistemic discipline*—the willingness to ask whether your information diet is varied enough to produce sound judgement. And this is where automation, simplicity, and systematisation begin to offer more than convenience—they offer insulation from ourselves. When your portfolio reflects a plan built on principles rather than predictions, the need to constantly affirm your views evaporates. The echo chamber dissolves. And in its place emerges a quieter, steadier confidence—one rooted not in being right, but in being resilient.

The next section of this chapter explores a close cousin of confirmation bias: the tendency to turn a few lucky breaks into self-serving folklore. It's one thing to overvalue opinions that mirror your own; it's another to turn those opinions into rules. Understanding how personalised myths distort investing behaviour will help us go deeper into the psychology of the DIY investor—and how to replace folklore with frameworks that last.

## The Trap of Personalised Folklore

Every investor begins with a strategy. For some, it's drawn from a book or a trusted mentor. For others, it's reverse-engineered from early wins. A trade goes well, a stock triples, a gut feeling pans out—and suddenly, a principle is born. "I always buy during earnings season." "Tech never fails over the long term." "Momentum is the only truth." These rules feel earned. They feel battle-tested. But more often than not, they're the result of survivorship bias and selective memory. What emerges is not a strategy—it's folklore: personalised, comforting, and deeply misleading.

This phenomenon isn't confined to amateurs or casual investors. It appears across experience levels and asset classes. What makes it so insidious is that it masquerades as wisdom. A trader makes money shorting airline stocks in the early pandemic panic. The lesson learned? Airlines are always overvalued and vulnerable. That rule, forged in crisis, calcifies into a belief. The market evolves, conditions change, but the belief persists—out of sync with data, yet clung to with conviction. The original trade becomes mythologised, its context forgotten. It's not treated as an isolated outcome, but as confirmation of the investor's unique insight. *This is how a narrative becomes a prison.*

Our brains are wired to seek causal stories, especially in noisy domains like markets. Nassim Nicholas Taleb called this the "narrative fallacy"—the tendency to explain random events with coherent, linear causes. When a trader makes a profitable decision, particularly early in their career, they instinctively search for reasons why it worked. But markets are probabilistic. Short-term results often contain more noise than signal. Yet humans dislike randomness. We retrofit meaning. And then we defend that meaning, sometimes for decades.

Consider the case of Marta, a school teacher in Leeds who began investing in 2018 after receiving an inheritance. She started cautiously, placing small amounts into a broad-market ETF. But a tip from a friend led her to invest in a small-cap renewable energy firm just before a sharp rally. "It felt like I'd unlocked something," she later said. "I wasn't just following the crowd—I was ahead of it." That win prompted her to chase similar trades in adjacent sectors. Over time, she reduced her ETF allocation and concentrated her holdings in speculative green tech. By 2022, her portfolio was down 40%. Still, she resisted rebalancing. "These companies are the future. I just need to wait it out."

Marta's experience is not about ignorance—it's about identity. The moment a rule becomes part of how someone sees themselves, it graduates from tactic to ideology. It's no longer just a method; it's a marker of insight, courage, even superiority. The investor is no longer adjusting to the market—they're defending a worldview. The rule is no longer tested; it's protected.

Much of this bias is retrospective. Investors recall their successful trades with greater clarity and importance than their losses. This selective memory inflates confidence and distorts pattern recognition. A 2011 study by Weber and Rasche found that investors systematically overestimated their past performance and attributed success to skill rather than luck. Crucially, this wasn't conscious lying—it was misremembering shaped by ego. *Over time, the remembered version of an investor's past becomes more instructive than the actual data.*

This is how folklore traps investors. It convinces them they're tailoring their strategy to themselves, when in fact, they're tying their hands with myth. The story of the lucky biotech trade becomes a rule about when to buy into clinical trials. The success with penny stocks becomes a belief in intuition over fundamentals. These aren't lessons—they're anecdotes pretending to be models.

Institutional investors guard against this through structured processes. They separate thesis from position size. They log their decisions with pre-mortems and scenario analysis. They subject ideas to external critique. But the DIY investor has no such guardrails. Their strategy evolves in a vacuum—self-reinforced, rarely challenged, and constantly affirmed by selective memory. Without deliberate reflection, a handful of early wins can distort decades of decision-making.

The trap of personalised folklore is particularly dangerous in bull markets. Rising tides conceal poor reasoning. When prices climb regardless of logic, even flawed theses get rewarded. Investors mistake correlation for causation and conflate timing luck with repeatable insight. Then, when markets correct, they're unprepared. The rulebook they've built—so intuitive in good times—proves useless under stress. Worse, they double down. "It worked before. I just need to wait longer." In doing so, they trade adaptability for stubbornness.

To escape this trap, investors must adopt a forensic attitude toward their own beliefs. Ask: *Where did this rule come from? What was the original context? Has the underlying logic held up over time?* Scrutinise the origin stories of your own convictions. When were they formed? Were they tested in different conditions? Would you believe them if someone else told you the same thing?

A practical intervention is the investing journal—not as a performance tracker, but as a record of reasoning. Each decision should be logged with rationale, alternative options considered, and what would falsify the thesis. Then, revisit those notes after 6 or 12 months. Not to punish mistakes, but to detect patterns of magical thinking. The goal is to separate what worked from why it worked. Without that separation, every profitable trade becomes a siren song, calling you further into dogma.

It's worth noting that even legendary investors fall into this trap. George Soros once spoke of his own fallibility as an edge: "I'm only rich because I know when I'm wrong." The key insight here is not humility—it's detachment. By refusing to romanticise his wins, Soros preserved his ability to pivot. In contrast, most retail investors become narrators of their own legend. Their portfolios are not portfolios—they're autobiographies.

This is also why automation offers a subtle but profound advantage. Automated investing systems don't believe in folklore. They don't mythologise the last bull run or anchor to the memory of a winning trade. They respond to data, not identity. By outsourcing rebalancing and risk management to a system, investors reduce the emotional gravity of past trades. Automation doesn't erase agency; it curates it—preventing folklore from metastasising into dogma.

Ultimately, the question is not whether you've invented rules, but whether you've tested them. A strategy is only as good as its ability to survive scrutiny. That scrutiny must be internal, honest, and frequent. It must ask: *Is this belief portable across contexts, or is it just a story I've told myself to feel smart?* Folklore feels safe. Frameworks feel slow. But only one of them scales.

The next section will explore how ego subtly fuels performance-chasing, anchoring investors to high points that distort their expectations. While folklore binds through memory, ego binds through identity. Both narrow an investor's field of vision. Learning to replace ego with evidence is the necessary next step for anyone seeking durability over drama.

## From Ego-Driven to Evidence-Based

Most investors don't set out to chase performance. They start with sensible intentions: save for retirement, grow wealth steadily, avoid major losses. But somewhere along the line, something shifts. A market rally they missed. A colleague bragging about a ten-bagger. A financial newsletter hinting at the "next Tesla." Suddenly, the modest strategy feels insufficient. The desire to be prudent transforms into the desire to be right—and then into the desire to be exceptional. This is how ego seeps into investing. Quietly, persistently, and often disguised as ambition.

Ego in markets rarely announces itself. It does not always look like arrogance or reckless speculation. It can look like diligence—refreshing charts hourly, scanning headlines, tweaking asset allocations weekly in the name of optimisation. But beneath this activity is often a psychological trap: the fear of underperforming, not just absolutely, but relatively—against peers, benchmarks, or even a prior version of oneself. The investor stops managing risk and starts managing status.

Performance chasing is the behavioural manifestation of that shift. It's the pattern of jumping between strategies, asset classes, or sectors based on recent winners. Momentum in prices creates momentum in psychology. If emerging markets are up, capital floods in. If AI stocks spike, portfolios reorient. This cycle is well documented in the data. Dalbar's research has consistently shown that the average equity investor underperforms the market not because of high fees, but because of poor timing—buying high and selling low in reaction to emotion, not evidence. *The mind, not the market, is the greatest source of drag.*

Why is it so difficult to resist? Because outperformance feels like a personal endorsement. A spike in portfolio value becomes proof of one's foresight. A clever stock pick that doubles is remembered for years—not for its impact on the portfolio, but for its validation of intelligence. The deeper danger is that this emotional high sets a new internal benchmark. Now, anything less than market-beating returns feels like failure. The baseline for satisfaction shifts. It's not enough to grow wealth—it must grow faster than others. Faster than last year. Faster than the market. Faster than expectations.

This mindset traps investors in a volatile loop: elation when they win, self-recrimination when they don't. Their portfolio becomes a scoreboard for their identity. And identity, once tethered to outcomes, is fragile. Market cycles are indifferent to effort or intent. Even the best strategies underperform at times. But ego doesn't tolerate drawdowns. It demands control, narrative, and perpetual validation. So the investor intervenes—at the worst possible moments. They tweak allocations, chase trends, or abandon diversified portfolios in favour of concentrated bets. What begins as self-expression ends as self-sabotage.

The antidote is not detachment, but discipline. Specifically: evidence-based investing. This doesn't mean becoming a passive purist or outsourcing all decisions to algorithms. It means grounding every decision—allocation, rebalancing, asset selection—in repeatable, empirically supported logic. It means replacing intuition with process. Preferences with probabilities. The investor must transition from *What do I think will happen?* to *What is the data likely to support over time?*

Take diversification. An ego-driven investor might scoff at broad exposure, viewing it as "diluted conviction." Why own the market when you can own the winners? But an evidence-based investor knows that diversification is not about hedging doubt—it's about absorbing uncertainty. It protects against the unknowable, not just the unlikely. Decades of academic literature—from Fama and French to behavioural economists—demonstrate that broad diversification reduces volatility and improves risk-adjusted returns.

Yet it requires surrendering the fantasy of superior insight. It requires humility.

Or consider rebalancing. The ego sees a rising asset and wants more of it. It feels unnatural to trim a winner and buy a laggard. But rebalancing enforces discipline: buy low, sell high. Not based on opinion, but on drift from a target allocation. Automated platforms execute this mechanically, removing emotion from the equation. Studies show that systematic rebalancing adds long-term value not because it predicts future returns, but because it keeps portfolios aligned with risk tolerance. It's not sexy—but it's effective.

The same applies to tax optimisation. An ego-driven investor might ignore the timing of gains, the placement of assets, or the use of tax-loss harvesting, focusing only on nominal returns. But the evidence-based investor understands that after-tax performance is what compounds. Strategies like asset location (placing tax-inefficient assets in sheltered accounts) or harvesting losses to offset gains are rarely exciting—but they add up, silently and reliably, year after year.

Behaviourally, this pivot requires reframing success. Ego asks: *Am I beating the market?* Evidence asks: *Am I following a strategy with a high probability of meeting my goals?* That subtle shift realigns attention from outperformance to sufficiency. It reduces anxiety, minimises FOMO, and increases the odds of sticking with a plan during inevitable volatility.

The key is to design a system that aligns with your actual temperament—not your aspirational identity. Investors often claim they're comfortable with risk—until markets fall 20%. Then they panic-sell. An evidence-based strategy begins with accurate self-assessment. Not just risk tolerance, but behavioural tolerance. How much volatility can you *emotionally withstand* without compromising your process? How frequently can you check your account without succumbing to action bias? These answers aren't found in financial theory—they're found in honest reflection.

Evidence-based investing also benefits from removing decisions from the moment of emotion. Rules must be made in calm periods, and followed during chaos. For example, predefining thresholds for rebalancing—say, when allocations drift 5%—eliminates the guesswork. Automating contributions and using target-date funds for retirement accounts ensure consistent progress without constant intervention. These structures aren't constraints—they're protections against our worst impulses.

What often surprises investors is how liberating this shift becomes. Ego-driven investing feels active and engaged, but it's cognitively exhausting. Every news event demands analysis. Every market movement invites reconsideration. Every underperformance bruises identity. In contrast, evidence-based investing feels slower—but it builds momentum. The investor stops trying to predict and starts implementing. They stop comparing and start compounding.

One of the best illustrations of this mindset is the difference between a gambler and a casino. The gambler bets on outcomes. The casino bets on systems. It knows the odds. It doesn't care about individual wins or losses—it cares about consistency over volume. Over thousands of iterations, edge wins. The evidence-based investor adopts the mindset of the casino—not by exploiting others, but by designing a process that doesn't require brilliance to succeed.

None of this means ego disappears entirely. It doesn't. It resurfaces, especially in bull markets. It whispers that maybe this time you *do* see something others don't. Maybe you should *just once* double down. That's why an evidence-based approach must be reinforced continuously—through journaling, through ritual, through accountability. Not to suppress confidence, but to channel it. *The goal is not to eliminate instinct, but to train it within a system that doesn't collapse under pressure.*

Ultimately, the move from ego to evidence is a rite of passage for serious investors. It marks the shift from speculation to stewardship. From chasing alpha to building a life. From short-term validation to long-term clarity. Markets will always tempt us with noise, novelty, and narrative. But those who succeed over decades are not the ones who know the future—they're the ones who know themselves, and trust in systems that work better than impulse. That's not defeat. That's wisdom.

# Chapter 7
# Global Platforms, Local Mindsets

In a world where capital flows instantaneously, data refreshes by the millisecond, and apps promise to make investing borderless, a stubborn truth persists: money is deeply cultural. Beneath the algorithms and glossy interfaces, behind the universality of spreadsheets and ETFs, every financial system carries the imprint of the society that produced it. For the modern investor, particularly one enticed by the frictionless appeal of robo-advisors, overlooking this truth is less an oversight than a risk.

What works in New York might be inefficient, even counterproductive, in Mumbai. A retirement strategy optimised for Californian tax law can be ill-suited for someone earning in Singapore while investing from Dubai. Yet global platforms often market simplicity as though it scales effortlessly across borders. As robo-advisors expand—from the structured regulatory environment of the United States into emerging markets with volatile tax frameworks—the pressing question shifts from which platform is "best" to which platform aligns with the investor's lived reality: where they earn, reside, and hold their values.

Consider the disparity between national investing landscapes. In the United States, long-term capital gains benefit from preferential tax treatment; index funds dominate portfolios; and financial advice centres on instruments such as IRAs and 401(k)s. In India, taxation is less forgiving, gold and real estate heavily influence allocation instincts, and instruments like the PPF continue to hold emotional sway. A platform optimised for US-based tax efficiency—Wealthfront or Betterment, for example—cannot seamlessly translate to a market where rules differ, financial literacy varies, and legal structures for digital asset management remain emergent. The tools may be global, but obligations and priorities remain firmly local.

The challenge is not merely technical; it is philosophical. Societies encode their attitudes toward money into investment systems.

Japan's collectivist culture shapes pension schemes prioritising stability over speculation. The United States elevates self-reliance, nurturing DIY investing. Germany's conservatism manifests in risk-averse investor behaviour and regulation. In the Middle East, Sharia-compliant finance defines entire classes of permissible investments. Platform design, in effect, mirrors national psyche. Deploying a tool designed for another financial culture is not neutral—it imports assumptions about risk, responsibility, and reward that may conflict with your context.

This is not a case for parochialism. On the contrary: for expats, remote workers, dual citizens, and digital nomads, complexity multiplies. A Canadian engineer living in the UAE, investing through a UK platform and retiring in Portugal, faces layers of exposure: currency risk, tax treaties, asset location, and cross-border execution. The question is not simply which platform executes trades, but which can navigate this web coherently.

The answer lies in understanding the alignment between platform philosophy and personal reality. Some platforms optimise domestic simplicity; others cater to international mobility. Some integrate ESG criteria per Western norms; others offer Sharia-compliant options or region-specific ethical investing. Some incorporate local tax logic; others assume a one-size-fits-all model. A sophisticated algorithm is meaningless if it models the wrong context.

This chapter invites the reader to step back—from assumptions rather than investing itself. It challenges the notion that globalised fintech is inherently superior, urging nuance instead. How does one remain globally connected yet locally grounded? How can investors avoid becoming unwitting arbitrageurs of their own portfolios, vulnerable to misalignments that silently erode returns?

We begin by interrogating the default bias embedded in many global platforms: the unspoken presumption that the US investing model is universal. It is not; it is dominant, scaled, and culturally exported, but its tax laws, risk frameworks, and retirement conventions may falter abroad. Algorithms optimised for US ETFs may, for instance, overexpose Indian investors to currency volatility or misclassify domestic assets due to incomplete data integration.

From there, we explore how national narratives shape investor psychology. In Asia, family-centric planning can outweigh individualist assumptions about retirement. In Africa, informal economies and institutional distrust reframe long-term saving behaviour. In Latin America, memories of inflation trauma influence risk preferences overlooked by Western platforms. Asking a platform to manage wealth is asking it to interpret fears, habits, and aspirations—an undertaking that fails if the model ignores local context.

We also examine the limitations of platform comparison tools. "Best robo-advisors" lists often privilege superficialities: app design, onboarding flows, headline fees. Real suitability is subtler. Does the platform integrate with local tax authorities? Support asset classes relevant to your goals? Handle multi-currency strategies without hidden slippage? Execute across jurisdictions as life circumstances demand?

Finally, we turn to the stateless investor: individuals whose work, citizenship, or residency does not fit neatly into a single jurisdiction. Whether an Indian developer in Berlin, a retiree earning in Thailand with UK assets, or a multinational entrepreneur hedging between the dollar and euro, such lives demand more than dashboards—they demand strategic coherence across fragmented systems.

Your passport is not your portfolio. Nor is your portfolio merely a technical instrument; it is a reflection of where you live financially, emotionally, and philosophically. This chapter does not prescribe a universal "best" platform. It offers tools for asking sharper questions, filtering options more effectively, and applying discernment with intentionality. Automation is not the threat—it is abstraction. The remedy is alignment: thoughtful, context-sensitive, value-driven alignment.

The aim here is not to overwhelm with technical minutiae but to cultivate strategic literacy. Tools are only as powerful as the questions guiding them. As robo-advisors flatten the mechanics of investing, the investor's task is to supply nuance—context, meaning, and values. That is the foundation of a portfolio that performs not only numerically, but in a way that honours life wherever it is lived.

## What Works in the U.S. Doesn't Always Work in India

The globalisation of fintech has created the illusion of universality—an impression that a platform, algorithm, or strategy that succeeds in one country can be transplanted wholesale into another. Nowhere is this misconception more consequential than in the rise of robo-advisors. Models born in the United States—such as Betterment or Wealthfront—project an aura of intelligent automation, low fees, tax efficiency, and behavioural discipline. And indeed, within the regulatory, tax, and cultural architecture of the United States, these platforms are powerful tools. But outside that framework—particularly in markets like India—the assumptions embedded in those models often misfire, creating distortions that range from inefficiency to risk.

At first glance, robo-advisors appear culturally agnostic. They operate through sleek interfaces, promise evidence-based asset allocation, and optimise portfolios using Nobel Prize-winning principles. But beneath the design lies an infrastructure deeply embedded in the U.S. ecosystem: low-cost index funds (especially ETFs), preferential treatment of long-term capital gains, a capital markets regime that rewards passive investing, and a behavioural model built on the premise of individual responsibility for retirement. Every feature, from automatic tax-loss harvesting to retirement account optimisation, assumes a particular policy, fiscal, and emotional environment. When exported to India, these assumptions are not just challenged—they often become liabilities.

Consider taxation. In the United States, long-term capital gains on equities are taxed at a lower rate than regular income, and tax-loss harvesting can be performed continuously with minimal friction. U.S.-based robo-advisors use this asymmetry to enhance after-tax returns, selling assets at a loss to offset gains elsewhere. In India, the structure is starkly different. Long-term capital gains above ₹1 lakh on equity instruments are taxed at 10%, and short-term gains at 15%, with few equivalents to the wash-sale rule or seamless carryover mechanisms found in the U.S. Moreover, India's tax code evolves more unpredictably, with retrospective amendments and shifting exemptions—conditions that frustrate algorithmic certainty. A tax strategy built for the U.S. may be inert or even harmful in the Indian context if it triggers unnecessary churn, fails to account for securities transaction tax (STT), or overlooks regime-specific exemptions.

The question of market maturity compounds this issue. The U.S. equity market is deep, liquid, and largely institutional. Passive investing thrives in such an environment because price discovery is efficient, and transaction costs are low. Indian markets, while increasingly mature, are still retail-driven, more volatile, and less index-centric. The NSE and BSE may offer broad-market indices like Nifty 50 or Sensex, but the availability of ultra-low-cost ETFs tracking them is limited compared to the U.S. Additionally, fund expenses in India—while improving—remain relatively high. A robo-advisor optimised for 0.04% U.S. ETFs may find its efficiency undermined in India by fund expense ratios that range closer to 0.5–1%. What's considered a negligible cost in one market can become a structural drag in another.

Then there's the regulatory terrain. U.S. robo-advisors operate under the oversight of the SEC and FINRA—regulators known for transparency, enforcement, and consistency. Indian counterparts function within SEBI's framework, which has made strides but remains a patchwork of evolving mandates, especially when it comes to algorithmic advice. For instance, SEBI only recently formalised rules around advisory versus distribution roles, leading to conflict-of-interest concerns and hybrid models. Many platforms in India still derive revenue from embedded commissions, unlike fee-only U.S. models. This affects the objectivity of advice and raises a philosophical question: *is the robo-advisor serving the user's interest or the fund house's shelf?* Automation may cloak this tension, but it does not resolve it.

Cultural psychology further complicates matters. U.S. investors are socialised into DIY financial responsibility. Retirement is self-funded; pensions are rare; and the 401(k) has become a secular rite of passage. In India, familial interdependence and informal support networks still shape financial behaviour. Parents often fund children's education and receive care in return during retirement. This creates a portfolio mindset that prioritises legacy, safety, and short-term liquidity over abstract optimisation. Robo-advisors that push aggressive equity allocations based on age-based heuristics can misalign dramatically with an investor's lived reality—particularly when that investor sees financial responsibility as collective, not individual. Risk tolerance questionnaires calibrated for Western psychology may misinterpret hesitation as irrationality, when it is in fact relational prudence.

Moreover, the asset class universe differs sharply. U.S. platforms are equity-dominant, sometimes including REITs or TIPS. Indian investors typically straddle a wider emotional asset spectrum: gold, fixed deposits, real estate, insurance-linked savings plans. A robo-advisor that fails to accommodate gold as a strategic holding—not just an alternative asset—misses a core cultural belief about security. Likewise, automated rebalancing that sells gold in favour of mid-cap equities may optimise on paper but violate the psychological covenant that many households place on tangible wealth. Effective strategy in such contexts must be not only mathematically sound but emotionally sustainable.

Even the semantics of financial planning vary. A U.S. investor may define a goal as "retire with $1 million by age 65." An Indian investor, facing inflation, currency devaluation, and inconsistent annuity markets, may struggle to articulate retirement needs numerically. Instead, goals are framed as "ensure daughter's wedding is covered," "buy a second flat in Pune," or "never be dependent." Robo-advisors that force quantification without cultural translation risk alienating users or, worse, guiding them with false precision.

Goal-based investing, when stripped of its human context, becomes mechanised projection—not planning.

This divergence has practical consequences. Importing a U.S.-centric robo-advisor into India without adaptation can result in mismatched portfolios, inefficient taxation, unmet expectations, and eventual abandonment. Some Indian platforms, such as Scripbox and Zerodha's Coin, have started addressing this localisation gap. They integrate tax treatment unique to Indian securities, account for market volatility through SIP-driven planning, and accommodate traditional instruments like EPF and PPF into overall portfolio advice. Yet even these platforms must continuously grapple with the tension between modernisation and localisation: how to scale automated intelligence without flattening cultural nuance.

The problem is not that U.S. strategies are flawed. It's that they are context-dependent. The allure of replicating a successful model across geographies is strong, especially in tech. But finance is not software. It is *embedded context.* Algorithms can calculate risk, but they cannot yet decode the sociology of savings. They can optimise returns, but they cannot replace the human narrative that defines what 'return' actually means in someone's life.

Global investors must therefore embrace a different paradigm: *platforms should be evaluated not by global best practices, but by local fit.* That means asking different questions: Does this robo-advisor model taxes correctly under my jurisdiction? Does it understand the instruments I actually use? Can it communicate in a language—both literal and cultural—that resonates with my understanding of risk and wealth?

There's also a call for regulators and entrepreneurs. If India is to become a serious player in the robo-advisory space, it must go beyond cloning global models and instead design systems that are built ground-up for Indian behaviour, tax logic, and financial anthropology. That includes designing tools that reflect multigenerational goals, complex risk appetites, and the hybrid reality of digital and physical asset coexistence.

For investors, the imperative is to move beyond the surface appeal of platform polish. A beautiful interface that masks misaligned strategy is more dangerous than a clunky interface that respects context. *Good investing is not about emulating what works elsewhere—it's about aligning with what works here, now, and for you.* The task is not to reject global wisdom, but to filter it through local discernment. That may not sound as seductive as universal automation—but it's far more likely to generate real-world results you can actually keep.

### "A Culture's Wealth Myth Becomes Your Strategy":

The architecture of wealth is never culturally neutral. It is shaped, often invisibly, by the stories we tell ourselves about money—what it's for, how it should be earned, who deserves it, and what we owe each other once we have it. These narratives, absorbed not from textbooks but from dinner tables, rituals, national policies, and subtle habits, form the scaffolding of our financial systems. When we choose an investment strategy, we are not only engaging with markets—we are, consciously or not, aligning ourselves with a specific cultural script about value, effort, and reward.

Robo-advisory platforms are built atop these cultural assumptions. While they market themselves as globally scalable, algorithmically rational, and empirically driven, the default logic behind their recommendations is rarely divorced from the national context in which they were designed. The underlying models may optimise for risk-adjusted returns, but the very definition of "risk", "adjustment", and even "return" is mediated by what a society values. The architecture of a robo-platform in the United States reflects different philosophical priorities than one in Japan or India, and the distinctions are not superficial. They are encoded deep in product design, asset allocation defaults, and assumptions about investor behaviour.

Consider, for instance, the American fixation on individual agency and retirement autonomy. U.S.-based robo platforms like Betterment and Wealthfront often assume a user profile of someone seeking early retirement, tax optimisation, and maximum control over personal financial destiny. The "goal-based" dashboards and self-paced onboarding interfaces are designed to flatter a narrative of independence. They rarely ask whether financial responsibility might be shared across extended family, or whether wealth might be pooled for intergenerational resilience rather than individual escape velocity. Contrast this with Indian robo-advisors like Scripbox, which reflect a different ethos—emphasising education goals, family security, and estate continuity as default objectives. Here, the unit of optimisation is not merely the individual investor, but the family network they are embedded within.

These philosophical divergences are not errors—they are strategic alignments. Financial technology does not emerge from a vacuum. It grows out of soil fertilised by cultural myths and institutional history. In Japan, for example, a culture of frugality, aversion to equity risk, and institutional conservatism is reflected in platforms that tilt toward conservative asset mixes, high cash buffers, and stronger guardrails against behavioural overreach. In contrast, American robo-advisors may lean more aggressively toward equities, assuming that time horizon and risk appetite will stretch to accommodate market cycles. Neither approach is objectively superior—but each reveals what a society believes about uncertainty, ambition, and control.

There is an unspoken danger when investors engage cross-border robo platforms without adjusting for these underlying assumptions. An Indian expatriate using a U.S. robo-advisor may unintentionally adopt a financial philosophy incompatible with their lived obligations—neglecting elder care, undervaluing gold as a cultural hedge, or optimising for an early retirement that isn't legally or socially feasible. Likewise, an American using a foreign platform may find themselves constrained by risk thresholds or liquidity assumptions that do not match their local tax regime or psychological tolerance. What looks like a convenient export of financial intelligence can, without scrutiny, become a quiet misalignment between platform logic and personal reality.

One of the most underappreciated aspects of designing a global portfolio is understanding how wealth itself is defined across contexts. In Western liberal economies, wealth is often synonymous with independence—the ability to retire early, to own property outright, to avoid relying on state systems. In many parts of Asia, by contrast, wealth is defined in relational terms: the ability to provide for aging parents, educate children without debt, or host a wedding that reflects social standing. These goals are not merely aesthetic differences; they drive fundamentally different patterns of savings, asset preference, and liquidity management. If your robo-advisor does not ask the right questions, it may optimise you away from your own priorities.

The language platforms use is also a tell. In Silicon Valley, wealth platforms often pitch themselves using metaphors of "freedom", "escape", or "taking control". The emotional proposition is autonomy. In India or Southeast Asia, robo-advisors are more likely to invoke duty, legacy, and continuity—the emotional proposition is stability. Even the visual design of the platform reveals these instincts. American dashboards tend toward minimalist interfaces that reinforce the myth of simplicity—fewer dials, more confidence. Indian platforms tend to use rich visuals, progress trackers for family goals, and educational content—reinforcing the idea that wealth is a long-term, guided journey.

When investors are unaware of these embedded values, they may misinterpret the tools they're using. A user may wonder why a platform's rebalancing logic doesn't match their expectations—not realising it's based on a volatility model more suited to a developed market index with deeper liquidity and more consistent monetary policy. Or they may find that tax-optimisation features recommended by a U.S. platform create unforeseen liabilities under a different jurisdiction. These are not technical glitches—they are mismatches between financial philosophy and personal reality, translated through software.

This makes the act of selecting a robo-advisor less about choosing the "best" algorithm and more about choosing an aligned worldview. Investors must learn to read between the product features to ask: *What kind of investor does this platform imagine I am? What does it assume I want to achieve, and on whose terms?* These questions are not abstract. They directly affect portfolio strategy—how much volatility is tolerated, which goals are prioritised, what assets are accessible, and what assumptions underpin the long-term forecast models.

The solution is not to dismiss foreign platforms outright, but to contextualise them. A globally mobile investor—say, an Indian national working in Singapore with a U.S. brokerage account—must become fluent in financial bilingualism. They need to understand the assumptions each platform makes, not just in terms of asset class availability or tax wrappers, but in terms of life philosophy. This fluency enables them to use platforms selectively—borrowing optimisation strategies without adopting worldviews wholesale.

This also calls for a more culturally intelligent financial literacy. Investors should learn to interrogate their own inherited money myths. Were they raised to believe that real estate is the safest investment because it's tangible? That debt is always dangerous, even when it's low-interest and tax-deductible? That diversification means owning stocks from ten local companies instead of one foreign ETF? These beliefs shape the mental model with which we approach automated investing. If unexamined, they can lead us to fight the algorithm instead of working with it.

Roboadvisory platforms are not just financial tools—they are embedded philosophies. Choosing one is not just a technical decision but a moral and cultural one. It reflects not only how you want to grow your money, but how you interpret risk, legacy, and security. To invest without cultural awareness is to mistake the map for the territory. The future of intelligent investing lies not in universalising strategy but in customising alignment. The best robo-advisor is not the one with the most features—it's the one that quietly reinforces your values while correcting your biases. And that begins by recognising that no algorithm is culturally neutral.

When we fail to see that, we risk letting someone else's story become our strategy. But when we choose with awareness, we move from unconscious imitation to informed integration—and from that, real financial clarity emerges.

## Choosing a Platform in Your Region—Beyond the Rankings –

The temptation to treat robo-advisors like consumer electronics—rankable, reviewable, and globally interchangeable—is understandable, but misguided. Most investors, especially those new to automated platforms, begin their research by typing phrases like "best robo-advisors 2025" into search engines. They encounter a wall of comparison charts and top-10 lists that reduce complex decisions into digestible, often superficial metrics: fees, returns, asset class options, or user interface design. But when it comes to choosing a platform that will influence your wealth trajectory over decades, this kind of checklist thinking is not only inadequate—it's dangerous. *A platform isn't just a service; it's an embedded framework for decision-making, and it must be interrogated not merely by its rankings but by its fit with your regional reality, personal psychology, and long-term goals.*

What most rankings fail to account for is that financial ecosystems are not harmonised across borders. A platform that excels in the U.S. market—designed around 401(k) integrations, capital gains tax optimisation, and specific regulatory assumptions—may be irrelevant, even harmful, to an investor in Singapore, Brazil, or India. Likewise, robo-advisors that work seamlessly in the UK may stumble when applied to jurisdictions with different withholding tax agreements or foreign investment restrictions. Regional differences in taxation, currency stability, inflation exposure, and even investor psychology demand a more sophisticated approach than global top-ten lists can provide.

Begin not with features, but with constraints. Ask: *What are the structural realities I live within?* In India, for instance, equity capital gains under ₹1 lakh are tax-free, and long-term holdings beyond one year are taxed at 10%—a setup that favours long-term growth strategies but penalises high-churn portfolios. In the UK, ISAs (Individual Savings Accounts) shield investors from both capital gains and dividend tax, changing the calculus of what "tax efficiency" even means. In the U.S., tax-loss harvesting plays a dominant role in platform differentiation—but that advantage is null if you are investing from a jurisdiction where those losses cannot be offset. If your robo-advisor doesn't align with your local tax regime, it may optimise the wrong metrics entirely.

Beyond taxation, there's the question of currency denomination and liquidity pathways. A platform that reports performance in USD but draws investments in INR introduces hidden volatility. Gains may look impressive on paper but be offset entirely by FX risk when the funds are needed. For an investor with future obligations—say, tuition fees in Australia or a mortgage in the UK—local currency exposure must be treated as a first-order consideration. Platforms that ignore this, or default to foreign currency assumptions, are not neutral; they are structurally misaligned. *The right platform is not the one that promises the highest yield; it is the one that understands what currency your future is denominated in.*

A more subtle but equally crucial factor is regulation. Some jurisdictions have strong consumer protections and compensation schemes for platform failure; others do not. European investors may rely on MiFID II standards for transparency and suitability, while Asian markets operate under looser interpretations of fiduciary responsibility. If a platform claims to be "regulated," that tells you very little without understanding which jurisdiction's definition of regulation is being applied. For example, a robo-advisor registered in the U.S. under SEC oversight must adhere to stringent disclosure rules. In contrast, an offshore platform operating out of an unregulated fintech hub may offer flashy features without legal recourse in case of mismanagement. Regional fit is not just about access—it's about accountability.

But the most under-examined aspect of platform choice lies in its philosophical orientation. Many robo-advisors are not merely neutral calculators—they carry implicit models of how you should behave. They are embedded with assumptions about rebalancing frequency, risk tolerance, and optimal asset allocation derived from historical data that may not reflect your economic reality. A platform trained on U.S. equity data from the last 40 years may assume high returns are your baseline expectation—leading it to recommend more aggressive allocations than are prudent in a slower-growing or more volatile market. *An algorithm trained on one geography's experience may misdiagnose your needs in another.*

This is where risk profiling deserves careful scrutiny. A five-question quiz about your willingness to stomach volatility is not a genuine psychological assessment. Nor is it robust against cultural context. In collectivist societies, for instance, financial decision-making is often shared. Risk tolerance is not individual but communal. A son may hesitate to invest aggressively because his parents depend on him financially. A daughter may accept high risk because she assumes she'll receive family help if things go wrong. If your platform's behavioural models don't capture these nuances, its asset allocation logic becomes unanchored. The result isn't just inefficiency—it's misrepresentation.

Some robo platforms are beginning to address this, offering "localised" portfolios and regional expertise. But this localisation often remains cosmetic—tweaks to asset weightings or added exposure to local debt instruments—without altering the foundational models that drive recommendations. More serious alignment comes only when a platform is built with deep understanding of local investor archetypes, legal infrastructure, tax law, and macroeconomic risk. The quality of a robo-advisor's engineering matters less than the integrity of its local interpretation.

And then there's the question of platform incentives. Review rankings rarely ask: *How does this company make money?* If the platform is fee-only, its incentives may be more transparent. But if it earns through revenue-sharing with mutual funds or ETFs, it may subtly steer you toward higher-cost products. In some markets, robo-advisors double as distributors—blurring the line between advisor and sales agent. This is particularly common in jurisdictions without strict separation between advice and execution. If you're not paying a platform directly, you should assume you're paying indirectly—and ask how that shapes the guidance you're receiving.

Investor support and educational framing also differ by region. Some platforms assume that users want to be educated along the way, providing just-in-time nudges or decision explainer content. Others assume that users want black-box simplicity and hide complexity entirely. There is no right answer—but there is a mismatch when an investor expects one experience and receives another. A platform that treats you as an informed co-pilot is a different creature from one that expects you to surrender control. Choose accordingly. *How a platform teaches you—or chooses not to—says a great deal about how it sees you.*

So how, then, should an intelligent investor evaluate platforms beyond rankings? Begin with grounded criteria:

Does the platform operate under a regulatory regime that protects your interests?

Are the default portfolios aligned with your tax jurisdiction and currency exposure?

Does the risk profiling reflect your actual constraints—not just your hypothetical bravado?

Are the platform's incentives clearly disclosed, and are product choices genuinely open architecture?

Does the platform assume a cultural model of wealth-building that mirrors or challenges your own—and in what ways?

The last question is not academic. If a platform's strategy assumes a linear, accumulation-focused life model—earn, invest, retire—it may misfire for those with nonlinear lives: freelancers, entrepreneurs, caretakers, or dual-income households spanning borders. In these cases, your portfolio needs to flex with irregular income, varied risk appetites, and shifting obligations. Most rankings don't assess this, because most rankings assume the user is an archetypal salaried professional in a developed market. You may not be.

Choosing a robo-advisor is not a one-time transaction. It is the acceptance of a long-term partnership with an algorithmic worldview. Treat it with the seriousness of any long-term relationship. That means interviewing the platform—testing how it responds to real constraints, probing its transparency, and evaluating how gracefully it handles complexity. If it buckles under the nuance of your financial life, it is not ready to steward your wealth.

And remember: the best platform is not the one that dazzles you with features or appears at the top of a list. It is the one that disappears into the background while consistently nudging you toward better decisions—decisions that are locally rational, personally relevant, and philosophically coherent. When a platform fits this well, you stop thinking of it as "a service" and start recognising it as a strategic ally. *That's the real benchmark of quality—alignment, not applause.*

## Your Passport Isn't Your Portfolio

*Offer insights for expats, global citizens, and those with multi-country income streams or taxation—how to keep simplicity amid complexity.*

When it comes to wealth management, many investors unconsciously treat their national identity as a default investment strategy. They invest where they live, assume their home currency is neutral, and regard tax policies as fixed constants. But for the globally mobile, this default becomes a dangerous oversimplification. A British citizen working in Singapore with U.S.-listed ETFs, Indian parents, and a child headed to university in Canada isn't an edge case anymore—this is the emerging face of a globally distributed investor class. And yet, most investment platforms, advisors, and even robo-advisors still behave as if every client is rooted in one legal system, one tax code, and one financial culture. The disconnect between the legal architecture of finance and the lived reality of globally mobile individuals is not just a logistical problem—it is a strategic blind spot.

To navigate this landscape effectively, the starting point must be a conceptual decoupling: *your citizenship is not your strategy*. The country listed on your passport may determine your visa status, but it does not—and should not—define your risk exposure, your asset allocation, or your tax posture. Understanding this distinction is the first step toward building a rational, robust, and location-agnostic investment setup.

For the modern global citizen, the challenge lies in reconciling three simultaneous identities: the tax resident (where you are legally liable), the financial actor (where your money works), and the life planner (where your goals reside). These are rarely unified. You may earn in dollars, spend in rupees, retire in Portugal, and leave an inheritance in yen. Managing this interplay is not a matter of clever spreadsheets—it requires a design philosophy that accepts *perpetual flux* as the baseline, not the exception.

Let's begin with taxes—not because they're thrilling, but because they quietly shape everything else. Consider the simple case of a British expat living in Dubai, investing in U.S.-domiciled ETFs. At first glance, it looks efficient: low-cost funds, strong global exposure, and no capital gains tax in the UAE. But buried in the U.S. tax code is the estate tax trap: non-resident aliens who hold over $60,000 in U.S. assets may be liable for up to 40% estate tax upon death. For a person with no U.S. ties besides their brokerage account, that's an astonishing liability. Now multiply this risk across jurisdictions. Indian investors holding mutual funds in Singapore may inadvertently trigger double taxation without the proper DTAA (Double Taxation Avoidance Agreement) protections. Canadians investing in PFICs (Passive Foreign Investment Companies) abroad encounter punitive tax treatments designed for corporate abuse but applied indiscriminately to individuals. These are not exotic edge cases—they're common outcomes of uninformed international investing.

The most efficient way to de-risk such entanglements is structural simplicity—not hyper-optimisation. Choose fund domiciles with tax treaties favourable to your residence or citizenship. Use platforms that offer multiple custodial options or multi-currency wallets. Avoid U.S.-domiciled ETFs if you're a non-resident alien; opt instead for UCITS funds domiciled in Ireland or Luxembourg, which offer tax neutrality and global diversification. If you don't understand the tax form your platform asks for (W-8BEN, CRS, FATCA, etc.), stop. Read it. These forms are not bureaucracy—they're boundary lines for international obligations.

Beyond taxation, the psychological cost of transnational investing is often underestimated. The more currencies and jurisdictions involved, the harder it becomes to perceive net progress. Imagine receiving income in euros, contributing to an NPS (National Pension Scheme) in India, investing via a Hong Kong brokerage, and paying rent in yen. Is your portfolio up? Down? Are you beating inflation? Beating which inflation? CPI-U in the U.S.? Retail inflation in India? The abstraction creeps in quietly until the numbers become untethered from lived experience. Without a framework, you don't just lose clarity—you lose conviction.

This is where automation, done correctly, becomes a philosophical commitment rather than just a convenience. Choose a robo-platform that allows currency diversification, not merely asset diversification. If you're an expat, prioritise platforms that offer tax reports aligned with your country of residence. Some platforms cater specifically to U.S. expats (e.g., Interactive Brokers with IRS-compliant reporting), while others focus on NRI needs (like Scripbox or Vested). Your goal is not simply to avoid tax drag, but to reduce *interpretive drag*—the exhaustion that comes from translating multiple dashboards into a coherent picture of your future.

To be clear: simplicity does not mean consolidation at all costs. Many expats are told to "keep everything in one place" for manageability, but this advice often overlooks regulatory asymmetries. A platform that is safe and regulated in one country may not be protected or even legal in another. Think about currency convertibility restrictions (India), capital controls (China), or fund access restrictions (U.S. mutual funds in the EU post-MiFID II). Global investing requires *platform pluralism*—an acceptance that the best setup may involve two or three interoperable platforms, each optimised for a distinct purpose: low-cost equity exposure, fixed income tax-efficiency, or retirement annuity planning.

Take the case of Zara, a dual citizen of Spain and Australia, working remotely in Thailand while investing via U.S.-based robo-advisors. Her income is in Thai baht, her base currency is AUD, but her retirement plan is euro-based. She wants to invest ethically, avoid U.S. estate tax, and keep her holdings accessible from multiple jurisdictions. Her solution? She uses a Luxembourg-domiciled ESG ETF portfolio via an EU-compliant robo-advisor, pays a Thai tax consultant annually to confirm non-residency thresholds, and keeps an Australian superannuation fund active as a fallback anchor. This isn't a workaround—it's a blueprint.

If there's a unifying principle for these globally fluid investors, it's this: *Design for agility, not for permanence.* Unlike your parents, you may live in five countries across three decades. Your portfolio must be built not around today's passport, but tomorrow's possibilities. This means favouring liquid, globally recognised instruments (ETFs over local mutual funds), choosing providers that support multi-jurisdictional reporting, and minimising hard-to-reverse commitments like annuities or tax-deferred structures that only work in one country.

And above all, keep your philosophy modular. Instead of seeking a universal platform or ideal domicile, segment your strategy: use one layer for core passive exposure (broad ETFs, globally diversified), a second for goal-based instruments (college fund, retirement, etc.), and a third for jurisdiction-specific needs (local tax-advantaged vehicles). This approach respects the complexity of global life while containing it within manageable boundaries.

Your portfolio should not be a hostage to your birthplace, nor a reflection of an advisor's default template. It should be a living structure—resilient, interpretable, and mobile. Because in a world where your job, your citizenship, and your family ties may span multiple continents, the idea that one brokerage account, one tax system, or one currency could serve as the stable ground for your financial life is not just naïve. It's obsolete.

# Chapter 8
# When Life Changes, Let Your Portfolio Adapt

No one disputes that life is in constant flux. Yet most investors overlook how profoundly these shifts recalibrate their financial identity. A promotion, a relocation, a medical diagnosis, the arrival of a child—these are not mere biographical footnotes. They subtly reshape risk tolerance, time horizons, and even the emotional scaffolding that underpins decision-making. And still, while fund performance and quarterly returns dominate attention, the far more consequential question—does your portfolio still reflect who you are today?—often goes unasked.

Traditionally, wealth management has fixated on assets. The wiser inquiry, however, begins with the self: what has changed in you? Most robo-advisors administer a single risk questionnaire at onboarding. Rarely do they follow up. Meanwhile, your life has shifted—new country, new currency, new career, new goals. The dissonance accumulates quietly. That 90% equities allocation you embraced at 28 may no longer suit your tolerance at 39, now balancing a mortgage, a toddler, and ageing parents. Numbers may remain stable, but the architecture is frozen in a previous chapter of your life. Reassessing your profile matters more than obsessing over returns.

Human events are not unknowable. Yet the financial industry, still tethered to industrial-age models of predictability, rarely incorporates these life signals into portfolio adaptation. Robo-advisors, by contrast, have the capability—both algorithmically and philosophically—to recognise these triggers, but only if the investor acknowledges them. The prompt for adjustment is not always market volatility. Sometimes it's a wedding; sometimes, a late-night search about fertility; sometimes, a calendar nudge to schedule a health check. These are the true risk vectors, often more consequential than GDP revisions or inflation reports.

This chapter begins by examining these invisible risk shifts—those imperceptible to volatility indices but palpable in daily routines. Life events quietly rewrite your financial posture, even when portfolios appear placid. We'll explore why aggressive allocations in youth are as much expressions of identity—confidence, ambition, ego—as they are calculations of time horizon. Over time, what appears cautious is not fear but dignity. A portfolio that softens with age does not signal surrender; it signals an evolved definition of success.

From theory, we move to confrontation: how does financial discipline hold up in crises? Market downturns test temperament, but personal crises—divorce, redundancy, illness—prove far more destabilising. They challenge not just allocation but trust in the systems you've built. Automated investments offer protection from panic; without them, the illusion of control collapses swiftly. We'll examine real cases: when market dips collide with personal vulnerability, why evidence-based design becomes indispensable and emotion so often misleading.

We'll also confront a frequently ignored dimension: the modelling effect. Legacy is often equated with estate planning and tax optimisation, yet the behaviours you display around investing may matter far more. Do children witness stress or calm? Dependents see strategy or reaction? A portfolio is not just a plan—it is a narrative unfolding in real time. And whether consciously or not, someone is observing and learning.

As the chapter unfolds, the focus is not simply on reallocation but on recalibrating your philosophy of control. Life does not pause for permission. The most effective investors build systems that interpret these shifts not as threats but as prompts for measured adjustment.

You do not need to respond to every market twitch. You must, however, respond to the evolving person who holds the portfolio. Because a portfolio is never a snapshot; it is a mirror. And the investors who excel are rarely those who forecast best—they are those who perceive when the person they designed the portfolio for no longer exists.

## Marriage, Parenthood, Relocation: Invisible Risk Shifts

The silent recalibration of risk does not happen in a spreadsheet. It begins the moment you say "I do," hold your child for the first time, or unlock the front door of a new home in an unfamiliar city. Life transitions—whether chosen or imposed—carry psychological ripples that quietly alter how we perceive uncertainty, commitment, and loss. Yet too many investors obsess over portfolio returns while ignoring the evolving assumptions that underpin them. The result? Portfolios that may remain technically diversified, but are emotionally misaligned.

What changes risk tolerance is not just market conditions, but human context. And unless your investment strategy is periodically re-anchored to that context, it becomes a museum exhibit of a former self—a frozen snapshot of an earlier identity.

*Risk tolerance is not static—it is situational, fluid, and deeply personal. Ignoring this truth is not discipline; it's detachment.*

Consider a young single professional with a steady job, high disposable income, and few obligations. For them, volatility may feel abstract—a line on a chart. The same individual, five years later, might be married, managing joint finances, and navigating parenthood. Market drawdowns no longer merely threaten future purchasing power; they now symbolise potential instability in the present. Rational or not, the emotional consequences change. If investment strategy doesn't adapt accordingly, the investor becomes a hostage to their own outdated assumptions.

Most financial questionnaires attempt to classify risk appetite in isolation—an overly sanitised process that often fails to account for the qualitative shifts in one's life architecture. Yet these shifts—not the S&P 500's latest performance—are often the real drivers of behavioural misalignment.

A 2021 behavioural finance study by the CFA Institute found that over 60% of individuals who self-identified as "aggressive" investors in their 20s downgraded to "moderate" or "conservative" within two years of starting a family—not due to losses, but due to a re-evaluation of what risk meant in their new context. The portfolios, however, often remained unchanged.

*Life transitions alter our risk capacity, not just our risk preference. The first is structural; the second is psychological. Both matter.*

Marriage, in particular, introduces a form of dual-accountability. The individual is no longer investing only for themselves, but with shared goals, timelines, and fears. Financial decisions now carry relational implications. A partner's lower risk appetite or past financial trauma can subtly influence allocation decisions, even when unspoken. The pretence of objective risk scoring begins to erode when confronted with real-life emotional variance between spouses.

Parenthood multiplies these effects. With children come new priorities—education planning, housing stability, and long-term legacy considerations. The very concept of "long-term investing" can become paradoxical. On one hand, parenthood increases the time horizon for wealth planning. On the other, it intensifies the need for short- and mid-term liquidity. This duality demands a portfolio structure that is both resilient and responsive, which only comes from re-examining assumptions—not just rebalancing assets.

Relocation—whether domestic or international—introduces another layer of complexity. Tax jurisdictions change. Cost of living changes. Income stability may vary. But more crucially, the psychological comfort with uncertainty often declines. The investor's social network, professional security, and sense of control may be diminished, and with it, their appetite for volatility. Robo-advisors that use static onboarding assessments may fail to capture this unless prompted. *A person who moves from New York to Singapore or from London to Nairobi doesn't merely change coordinates—they change context. Risk tolerance should follow.*

To illustrate this point, consider a case study from a global wealth platform that analysed investor behaviour across life events. It found that clients who had not updated their profiles post-major life events were three times more likely to override automated recommendations manually, often reacting emotionally to short-term market noise. Those who proactively revisited their risk profiles after key transitions exhibited steadier behaviour, higher portfolio adherence, and lower incidence of panic selling.

*Updating your risk profile is not a formality—it's an act of financial self-awareness.*

Most robo-advisory platforms allow users to revisit their goals and reclassify their risk appetite. But few prompt this behaviour unless the user initiates it. This is where a hybrid ritual—half automation, half reflection—can play a decisive role.

The optimal investor, paradoxically, is not the one who "sets and forgets," nor the one who checks their portfolio weekly. It is the one who integrates *structured check-ins* after meaningful life events. A wedding, the birth of a child, a new mortgage, or a geographic move—each of these should serve as a prompt not for tactical reallocation, but for strategic recalibration.

Why does this matter so much? Because mismatch—not market volatility—is what often causes regret. When a portfolio no longer reflects the investor's real-world reality, decisions become emotionally incoherent. Fear and greed take over not because the market changes, but because the investor's life did—and the portfolio didn't notice.

There's a broader philosophical point here too. Most people approach investing as a technical discipline—what's the asset mix? What's the return forecast? But *investing is also autobiographical.* It reflects who you are, what you value, and what trade-offs you're willing to accept. When life changes, so does your story. And your portfolio must be fluent enough to keep up.

Even the most robust automated portfolios require periodic human input to remain aligned. This isn't a failure of automation—it's a recognition of human evolution. Just as pilots rely on autopilot for stability but take control during turbulence or landing, so too must investors know when to re-engage—not to micromanage, but to realign.

So, the next time you think about checking your returns, pause. Ask instead: *Have I changed in a way that my portfolio hasn't noticed?* If the answer is yes, the most important investment decision you'll make this year might not be buying or selling an asset—it might be reassessing your own appetite for risk, in light of who you've become.

Let the data drive the engine. But let your evolving self revise the map.

## From Aggressive to Gentle: The Arc of Aging Portfolios:

The common assumption in investment discourse is that risk tolerance declines with age because older investors are more cautious, more fragile, and more fearful. But this framing is both simplistic and subtly ageist. What it overlooks is that risk tolerance doesn't simply erode with age—it evolves with perspective. The shift from aggressive to gentle portfolios isn't a retreat from boldness. It's a conscious recalibration—a reflection of matured priorities, sharpened self-awareness, and a hard-earned understanding of what money is actually for. Far from signalling a loss of edge, this pivot represents a refinement of purpose.

The financial industry often packages ageing with condescension: a countdown to capital preservation, annuities, and "safe" instruments, as if one's investment life is inevitably doomed to a quiet shuffle offstage. But in reality, older investors are not less capable of risk—they are more selective with it. With time, people become less interested in outperforming others and more focused on aligning their capital with what matters. This is not cowardice. It is clarity.

A portfolio's evolution over time should mirror the arc of an investor's life. In youth, risk is often tolerated because the stakes feel abstract: retirement is decades away, the idea of losing capital doesn't yet collide with lived experience, and ambition masquerades as strategy. A 25-year-old's desire to invest aggressively is often not a carefully considered posture—it is a mix of optimism, exposure to online investing culture, and the psychological safety net of time.

And in most cases, this is entirely appropriate. Time horizon, after all, is the greatest buffer against volatility.

But as investors enter midlife and beyond, several inflection points quietly reshape the calculus. They are rarely signposted by markets or brokers, but they are deeply human: a parent's declining health, a child's university fees, an unexpected redundancy, a reassessment of legacy. These events don't just alter your expenses—they alter your emotional attachment to money. They shift your tolerance not because you're becoming more fearful, but because you're becoming more aware of what your portfolio underwrites: the life you've built, the people who rely on you, the principles you want to preserve. *Risk becomes more concrete—and therefore, more curated.*

This is where the role of automation can be both powerful and dangerous. Many robo-advisors adjust for age-based glide paths—gently moving users into more conservative allocations as they age. But if these shifts are treated as default formulas rather than reflections of personal evolution, they can become mechanical approximations of what should be a reflective act. A 60-year-old entrepreneur who has just sold a business may have a higher risk capacity than a 45-year-old with a mortgage and two dependents. The variable isn't just age—it's *context.*

What automation does brilliantly, however, is reduce emotional interference. It prevents the ego from clinging to the myth that "I'm still the same investor I was at 30." It enforces structure over sentimentality. Left to their own devices, many DIY investors struggle to adapt their portfolios to ageing not because they lack tools—but because they resist the symbolism. They equate a conservative allocation with surrender, as if reducing equity exposure means abandoning ambition. But smart investors don't view gentler portfolios as settling for less. They understand that *financial sophistication often involves subtraction, not expansion.*

Consider a case study: a couple in their early 60s, both academics, with no debt and a modest pension stream expected to activate within five years. They've spent decades in diversified equity portfolios, and their returns have been consistently strong. Yet after witnessing friends struggle with medical costs and navigating long-term care decisions for ageing parents, they choose to shift 40% of their holdings into short-duration bonds and international dividend funds. Not because they fear markets—but because they value predictability in the near term. The decision is not reactive. It is rational. And it preserves their dignity.

This is the maturity of financial design—when asset allocation becomes less about outperforming the market and more about aligning with the contours of one's actual life. And this maturity is not reserved for the elderly. Even younger investors can adopt a forward-looking discipline by asking: *How will this portfolio need to evolve not just as markets shift, but as I do?*

The psychological side of this arc cannot be overstated. Transitioning from aggressive to gentle is not only a matter of spreadsheets—it's a shift in self-conception. For many investors, especially those whose identity has been tied to high returns, volatility-tolerance, or speculative wins, the idea of reducing equity exposure can feel like abandoning a part of themselves. But it is precisely this moment that separates the speculator from the strategist. Maturing portfolios invite you to see investing not as a theatre of self-expression, but as a tool for grounded stewardship.

This also requires honesty about *return expectations*. A portfolio designed for decumulation—or lower risk tolerance—should not be held to the same performance yardstick as a high-growth accumulation model. This is where many DIY investors falter: they soften their allocation, yet continue benchmarking themselves against the S&P 500 or their more aggressive peers. The result is dissatisfaction not with actual outcomes, but with misaligned comparisons. Wise investors adjust not only their risk, but their definition of success.

Robo-advisors can support this transition effectively, provided they are calibrated to meaningful inputs. Age is an imperfect proxy. What matters more is whether the algorithm regularly incorporates *life updates*: anticipated retirement dates, income changes, shifting priorities, liquidity needs. A static profile does not capture a dynamic life. The best automated platforms allow gentle nudges—a re-profile survey every 12 to 24 months—to ensure that the glide path reflects the investor's true trajectory, not just their date of birth.

Philosophically, there is beauty in the idea that investment identity matures with age. One need not "retire" from investing; rather, they transition from *accumulating for the unknown* to *curating for the known.* The act becomes more precise. More meaningful. Instead of asking "What will earn the most?", the question becomes "What serves my life best now?" This is not timidity. This is clarity distilled.

We must abandon the idea that gentler portfolios are inherently less intelligent or less ambitious. On the contrary, they reflect a different kind of ambition: the ambition to live well with what one has built, to sleep without anxiety, to provide without gambling, to design without drama. Financial maturity is the shift from velocity to alignment.

By reframing the arc of ageing portfolios as a *progression* rather than a retreat, we restore dignity to the process. The portfolio doesn't shrink in ambition—it deepens in purpose. It stops chasing the market and starts serving the person. And that is not a downgrade. It's a masterstroke.

## Crisis as a Test of Trust:

The true measure of an investment strategy is not how it performs in placid waters, but how it behaves when the tide recedes and the currents surge. Most investors do not test their mettle during bull markets; they simply ride the prevailing optimism. The real test—emotional, behavioural, and strategic—emerges during crises: market crashes, sudden job losses, medical emergencies, or geopolitical upheavals. These moments do not just challenge portfolio returns; they challenge our relationship with risk, uncertainty, and control. It is in this context that the resilience of algorithmic investing becomes not merely a technical advantage, but a psychological safeguard.

The global financial crisis of 2008, the pandemic-induced panic of March 2020, and more localised disruptions—such as Brexit for UK investors or demonetisation in India—have all exposed a common vulnerability: human instinct under pressure is a poor portfolio manager. We chase news cycles, overvalue recent losses, anchor to pre-crisis highs, and scramble for control in the face of volatility. *Robo-advisors, in contrast, do not blink.* They rebalance, reinvest, and remain indifferent to headline drama. This dispassionate discipline is not a bug of automation—it is its core feature.

During the COVID-19 market crash, for instance, a swathe of DIY investors fled to cash at the bottom, locking in losses that would have been reversed had they stayed put. Meanwhile, clients on platforms like Betterment or Nutmeg saw their portfolios quietly rebalanced. As equities fell and bonds held steady, algorithms increased equity allocations to maintain target risk levels—*buying low by design.* When the markets recovered within months, the gap between algorithmic and emotional investing became more than philosophical. It became measurable in returns.

But it is not only financial markets that cause upheaval. A health emergency—say, a cancer diagnosis in the family—or a sudden layoff has the power to derail even the most carefully composed investment intentions. The urgency of the situation often compels people to make reactive choices: liquidate a fund, delay a planned investment, or suspend contributions "until things stabilise." Yet these are precisely the junctures where pre-committed strategies, structured automation, and delegated discipline are most protective. A robo-advisor, unburdened by your immediate fears, continues executing a long-term plan that your future self will be grateful for.

This is not to say that automation renders human involvement obsolete. Rather, it *recalibrates the human role.* In times of crisis, the investor's job is not to intervene impulsively, but to *intelligently assess whether their circumstances have structurally changed.* Has the timeline for financial goals shifted? Has the risk tolerance genuinely decreased due to new obligations or constraints? If not, then most adjustments are emotional reactions in disguise. Algorithms can't feel fear—and that is their strength—but neither can they understand context. The investor must provide that context and then let the machine execute with precision.

Consider the case of Rajesh, a 43-year-old software consultant living between Singapore and Mumbai. In mid-2021, his mother was diagnosed with a neurological condition requiring long-term care. The medical costs were daunting, and his first instinct was to redeem part of his equity fund in India, which had recently doubled in value. But upon consulting his robo-advisor's platform and financial planner, he was reminded that his emergency fund was sufficient and his equity exposure—being already dialled down due to his risk profile—was not excessive. He left the portfolio intact, avoided capital gains tax, and used the automated withdrawal facility to generate monthly liquidity from his bond allocations. His mother received the care. His long-term plan stayed intact. *Resilience is not about rigidity; it is about design.*

Crises also reveal the silent risk embedded in manual management: *the illusion of control.* When we self-manage portfolios, we often tell ourselves that staying informed equates to being prepared. But during major events, information overwhelms rather than clarifies. The torrent of expert opinions, social media speculation, and contradictory forecasts paralyses even seasoned investors. Robo-advisors sidestep this trap entirely. They do not require certainty—they operate on algorithms that adjust to probabilistic changes, not dramatic headlines. This form of adaptive rationality is deeply underappreciated.

Even professional money managers, armed with data rooms and research teams, routinely fail to outperform passive indexes during market crises. What hope, then, for the retail investor monitoring CNBC in between meetings? The comparative advantage lies not in superior forecasting, but in superior *behavioural engineering.* The architecture of automated investing is built around this premise: humans are bad at crisis response; machines, if pre-programmed wisely, are not.

Of course, the resilience of robo-advisors is only as robust as the design of their protocols. Not all automation is created equal. Some platforms paused withdrawals or froze rebalancing during March 2020, exposing gaps in their underlying architecture. Others executed flawlessly, precisely because they were built not just for average-case efficiency, but for worst-case durability. *Choosing the right platform, therefore, is not merely a function of fees or features, but of crisis readiness.*

This raises a subtle but profound question: *what does trust in a financial system actually mean?* Is it faith in its predictive power, or in its procedural integrity? For many investors, the 2022–23 inflation shock tested their belief in modern monetary theory, bond markets, and central banks. But those who had pre-set, globally diversified portfolios experienced volatility within bounded expectations. There was no need to overhaul strategy—only to observe that temporary drawdowns were part of the design. Trust, in this context, is not blind faith. It is a choice to rely on systems that are smarter than your fear.

Behavioural finance has repeatedly shown that most investors are *risk-averse* in theory but *loss-averse* in practice. During stable times, people claim comfort with a 20% drop—until one occurs. Then comes the cascade of regret, second-guessing, and reactionary overcorrection. A well-designed robo-advisor system preempts this by gradually calibrating exposure through lifecycle models or glide paths. It doesn't just rebalance; it inoculates. And for those who choose to check their dashboards during a crisis, they see not chaos, but coherence. That visibility itself becomes a source of calm.

There is also a deeper philosophical lesson here. Crises are not merely interruptions to an otherwise smooth financial life. They are the *normative stress tests* that reveal whether your strategy is *designed for your real life*, or merely optimised for spreadsheet projections. The robo-advisor model—at its best—does not promise immunity from loss, but *a disciplined structure for recovery*. And over the long term, this difference compounds.

Some critics argue that automation dulls intuition or fosters detachment. But the opposite is true when implemented correctly. Delegating execution to algorithms frees the human investor to focus on the qualitative aspects of financial life: re-evaluating goals, reflecting on priorities, adjusting values. Crises are not only market events; they are existential inflection points. A spouse's death, a startup failure, a war in your home country—these demand a response, but not necessarily a reaction. *Strategy begins with clarity, not motion.*

Ultimately, crisis resilience is not about predicting shocks but surviving them *with integrity to your values*. The investor who has planned well through automation, calibrated their risk exposure, and left room for human discretion where it matters, emerges from crisis not merely intact—but improved. Trust in this context is not the absence of fear, but the presence of a framework strong enough to contain it.

And perhaps that is the highest promise of robo-advisors—not that they will make you rich faster, but that they will *stop you from becoming your own worst enemy when it matters most*. The algorithms do not care about your panic—but they care for your plan. And when your world wobbles, that steadiness is no small thing.

## Legacy Isn't Just Estate Planning –

Legacy is a concept that extends far beyond the legal formalities of estate planning. It is a reflection of the values we embody, the lessons we impart, and the influence we leave on those who come after us. When contemplating our financial legacy, the conversation often defaults to wills, trusts, and the distribution of assets. Yet, the true power of legacy lies not merely in *what* we pass on, but in *how* we have stewarded our wealth and modelled financial behaviour throughout our lives. This subtle yet profound shift—from an exclusively transactional view to a values-centred perspective—reshapes our approach to investing, enriching both our financial strategies and our enduring impact.

At its core, investing is not simply about accumulation but about alignment. The choices we make in portfolio construction, risk tolerance, and even the platforms we select broadcast messages about what we prioritize: stability or growth, short-term gain or long-term sustainability, personal gain or social responsibility. Each investment decision reverberates beyond numerical returns; it signals to family, community, and society the financial ethics we champion. For instance, an investor who opts for sustainable funds or impact investing communicates a commitment to environmental stewardship and social equity. This decision is an act of legacy, articulating a worldview that transcends mere dollars.

Consider the story of Sarah, a philanthropist in her sixties who deliberately chose to channel a significant portion of her portfolio into ESG (Environmental, Social, and Governance) funds. For Sarah, legacy was not about leaving an inheritance untouched but about demonstrating that capital can be a force for good. Her family, observing this commitment, has since adopted more conscientious financial practices, showing how legacy operates as behavioural inheritance, not just financial transfer. The investment strategy, in this case, became a language through which values were communicated and cultivated.

This interplay between investing and legacy invites critical reflection on the *narratives* we construct around money within our families. Often, financial habits and attitudes are inherited unconsciously—stories of scarcity, risk aversion, or excessive risk-taking are passed down like heirlooms. By engaging intentionally with our investing strategies, we disrupt unproductive cycles and foster a legacy of financial literacy, resilience, and mindfulness. The deliberate structuring of one's portfolio thus becomes an opportunity to teach, to inspire, and to embed principles that serve not just wealth preservation, but personal and communal flourishing.

Moreover, the concept of legacy challenges us to reconcile the tension between control and surrender. While estate planning focuses on precise control over asset distribution, the investment journey is about embracing uncertainty with purpose. Markets will fluctuate; strategies will evolve. The financial legacy that matters is one that models adaptability and patience—the recognition that wealth, like life, is dynamic. Teaching heirs to respect this fluidity and to avoid impulsive reactions to market volatility is arguably the most valuable inheritance an investor can provide.

This perspective also urges a reconsideration of time horizons in portfolio design. Traditional financial advice often emphasises risk reduction with age, yet a legacy-minded approach invites a nuanced understanding of longevity—not just of lifespan but of influence.

Some investors may choose to maintain growth-oriented allocations longer, intending to fund multigenerational projects or enduring philanthropic initiatives. Others may prioritise steady income streams to support family members' evolving needs, thus modelling a legacy of care and stability. The point is that investment decisions become expressions of intention about the future, serving as tangible manifestations of legacy.

Ethical reflection is intrinsic to this dialogue. Investing is never value-neutral. Whether consciously or unconsciously, each portfolio endorses certain industries, business practices, and societal impacts. By scrutinising these alignments, investors assert agency over their legacy's moral dimension. This self-awareness resists the reduction of wealth to mere numbers and reconnects finance to its human purpose. Legacy, therefore, is an invitation to infuse investing with conscience, encouraging strategies that are not only profitable but principled.

Yet, legacy's reach extends beyond family and philanthropy. In an interconnected world, our investing choices signal affiliations with broader societal movements. For example, divesting from fossil fuels can be a public statement, inspiring others to reconsider their financial commitments. Conversely, unchecked pursuit of profit at any cost risks perpetuating cycles of inequality and environmental degradation. Thus, legacy compels investors to weigh their portfolios' footprints and recognise the power of capital as a social agent.

In practical terms, crafting a legacy-minded investing strategy requires intentionality in goal-setting, asset allocation, and communication. This involves conversations with financial advisors that transcend quarterly returns and focus instead on aligning strategy with deeply held values. It requires documenting intentions through mission statements or ethical guidelines embedded within investment mandates. Furthermore, it demands ongoing reflection, revisiting and revising strategies as life circumstances and societal contexts evolve.

Ultimately, legacy in investing is a living construct. It invites investors to move from transactional interactions with money to transformational relationships with wealth. It elevates financial planning to a moral and philosophical exercise—one that shapes not only what is left behind but who we are remembered to be. By approaching investing as a medium of legacy, we cultivate a richer, more coherent narrative of wealth—one that honours past, present, and future in equal measure.

This understanding compels us to ask: *What story does your portfolio tell?* More importantly, *what story do you want it to tell?* Legacy, when conceived beyond estate planning, becomes a canvas on which to paint the values, hopes, and responsibilities that define a life well-lived and a future well-begun.

# Chapter 9
# A Simpler Portfolio, A Richer Life

Wealth, as it is commonly pursued, is often treated as a destination—a target defined by numbers, acquisitions, and ever-escalating benchmarks. Yet this relentless chase obscures a subtler reality: wealth is rarely the endpoint. More often, it emerges as the byproduct of a life carefully structured, thoughtfully lived. When we free investing from the narrow confines of "getting rich," a different perspective unfolds. Investments become instruments for creating space—space for meaningful work, for sustaining relationships, for rest that actually replenishes. Viewed this way, true richness is less about constant activity and more about intentional stillness and simplicity.

Modern finance glorifies movement: trades executed, portfolios rebalanced, market trends scrutinised in real time. But beneath this relentless rhythm lies an alternative strategy—one that privileges quiet. The ability to resist the almost irresistible urge to act, to tolerate boredom in service of long-term goals, is itself a competitive advantage. Silence, here, is not inertia but a deliberate tactic, rooted in patience. It is the discipline to let the system work, to let compounding accrue, and to avoid the errors that emerge from compulsive intervention. In this sense, stillness is a form of mastery.

Automation and systemisation become natural allies. Some may fear that automating decisions strips away human judgement, leaving cold algorithms in control. Yet, paradoxically, what is automated liberates our humanity. By removing repetitive tasks and constant monitoring, we reclaim attention and emotional energy, allowing life beyond markets to flourish. Investment, once a source of anxiety and distraction, quietly supports a fuller existence. The more the system hums reliably in the background, the more our cognitive bandwidth opens to creativity, connection, and contemplation.

The central insight of this chapter is deceptively simple: investing is not a separate arena of life. It is an extension of life itself, a tool to serve broader purposes rather than an end in isolation. Shifting focus from charts and balances to human experience—how we spend time, nurture relationships, and cultivate meaning—transforms portfolios into instruments of intentional living. Simplicity, rather than constraining, becomes liberating: a means to clear mental space and allow richness to flourish unencumbered by noise.

Throughout this chapter, readers will encounter frameworks that dismantle common myths of wealth and perpetual action. Illustrative examples reveal how quiet, deliberate approaches consistently outperform frenetic ones. Thoughtful prompts encourage alignment between investing and values, transforming portfolios from mechanical spreadsheets into expressions of purpose.

Ultimately, this is a call to reclaim control—not through incessant intervention, but through disciplined restraint; not by chasing every market tremor, but by cultivating the calm that allows wise decisions and a life well-lived. In a world enthralled by speed and noise, the richest lives may indeed emerge from the simplest portfolios.

## Wealth Is a Byproduct, Not a Goal –

Wealth is often framed as the destination of investing—a goal to be pursued with singular focus and relentless ambition. This narrative, while pervasive, misses a profound point: wealth is not the endpoint but the byproduct of a life thoughtfully designed. When we position investing as merely a path to "getting rich," we risk overlooking what truly matters—the creation of space for meaningful work, nourishing relationships, and restorative rest. This reframing challenges the conventional wisdom, inviting us to reconsider not only our financial strategies but the deeper purpose they serve.

The notion of wealth as a byproduct aligns with contemporary behavioural finance and psychological research, which emphasises that *human flourishing cannot be reduced to monetary accumulation*. Studies show that beyond a certain threshold, increased wealth correlates weakly with happiness or life satisfaction. Instead, the quality of time, freedom from financial anxiety, and the ability to engage deeply with personal values contribute far more to well-being. Investing, therefore, should be understood as a means to these ends—not an end in itself.

Consider the example of professionals who invest aggressively with the explicit goal of early retirement. While this goal is laudable, many report that the journey becomes all-consuming: constant market monitoring, stress over short-term fluctuations, and an unyielding pursuit of returns crowd out the very experiences they sought. This phenomenon, often termed *"financial burnout,"* reveals the paradox of wealth as a goal: the chase can consume life rather than enrich it. In contrast, those who view wealth as *a tool to create time and freedom* often report greater peace and satisfaction—even if their portfolio growth is steadier and less spectacular.

Central to this perspective is the concept of *"financial space"*—the freedom that wealth enables. Financial space manifests as the ability to choose how one spends time: pursuing creative projects without the pressure of immediate income, investing in relationships without financial strain, or simply resting without guilt. This shifts the narrative from accumulation to cultivation. Investing becomes an act of stewardship over one's future freedom, not a frantic sprint to a numeric target.

Modern investing platforms and robo-advisors, with their emphasis on automation and passive strategies, support this shift. By reducing the need for constant intervention, they enable investors to step back from the noise and complexity of markets. This, in turn, facilitates a lifestyle where investing is integrated seamlessly into a broader life plan rather than dominating it. *The calm generated by this approach is itself a form of wealth,* one that protects against the psychological toll of hyperactivity and impulsivity.

Yet embracing wealth as a byproduct requires a recalibration of our internal metrics. Success in investing must be redefined beyond portfolio value to include *alignment with personal values and life goals*. This involves translating abstract ambitions like "financial independence" into concrete, emotionally resonant milestones—time spent with family, creative fulfilment, travel, or community engagement. By doing so, the portfolio becomes a reflection of the investor's identity and priorities, rather than a detached ledger of gains and losses.

Philosophically, this approach echoes the wisdom of ancient thinkers who warned against confusing means with ends. Aristotle's notion of *eudaimonia*, or flourishing, underscores that external goods—money included—are valuable only insofar as they serve a life of virtue and purpose. Investing, when understood in this light, becomes an instrument of flourishing rather than a driver of greed or anxiety.

This reframing also invites ethical reflection. When wealth is pursued as a goal unto itself, decisions may skew toward short-termism, risk-taking beyond one's means, or neglect of social responsibility. Viewing wealth as a byproduct encourages stewardship—consideration of how investing impacts not only oneself but future generations and society at large. This broader vision fosters a *more sustainable, conscientious investment ethos.*

Practical applications of this philosophy are evident in the growing popularity of socially responsible investing (SRI) and environmental, social, and governance (ESG) criteria. Investors are increasingly motivated by the desire to align their capital with their values, affirming that wealth creation is inseparable from ethical considerations and the cultivation of a meaningful legacy.

For the intelligent, time-conscious reader, this shift demands more than a change in strategy—it requires a *paradigm shift in mindset.* Rather than measuring success by volatility or returns alone, investors are encouraged to cultivate patience, restraint, and clarity about their true motivations. This mindset fosters resilience against market shocks and emotional turbulence, anchoring investing within a broader life context.

Ultimately, recognising wealth as a byproduct invites a richer, more humane approach to finance. It frees individuals from the trap of endless striving and reconnects them to the fundamental human needs that money alone cannot satisfy. This chapter offers not only a critique of prevailing narratives but a hopeful, practical vision for investing that serves life rather than overwhelms it.

Every paragraph here aims to illuminate the path from frantic accumulation to deliberate abundance—where wealth is the quiet enabler of a life filled with purpose, connection, and rest. This is the heart of intelligent investing in the modern age: not a race to the finish line, but the cultivation of space for what matters most.

## Silence as a Financial Strategy –

The relentless drive to constantly engage with the financial markets has become a defining feature of modern investing culture. With the proliferation of real-time data feeds, push notifications, and algorithmic trading platforms, many investors find themselves trapped in an endless cycle of monitoring, tweaking, and reacting. Yet beneath this frenetic activity lies a paradox: *sometimes the most effective financial strategy is silence.* Reclaiming boredom, quiet, and deliberate inaction may seem counterintuitive, even radical, but these qualities embody a profound wisdom increasingly validated by both research and practical outcomes. This subchapter argues for silence as a financial strategy—a disciplined retreat from the noise that allows for clarity, patience, and resilience in an unpredictable market environment.

The urge to be constantly "doing" in finance is often conflated with empowerment. Each trade executed, each portfolio reallocation, and every new market insight consumed offers a fleeting sense of control. However, behavioural finance repeatedly shows how *excessive intervention undermines investment outcomes*. This phenomenon—known as the *activity bias*—stems from deeply ingrained cognitive biases like overconfidence and the illusion of control. Investors mistake action for progress, overlooking the cost of reactionary decisions driven by emotion rather than reason. Empirical evidence underscores this: numerous studies demonstrate that investors who trade less frequently and adhere to a consistent strategy outperform those who chase market movements or react impulsively to short-term volatility.

The concept of silence in investing is not synonymous with passivity or neglect. Rather, it entails *cultivating the capacity to resist impulsive actions*, to embrace moments of stillness, and to trust the underlying investment process. This aligns with the wisdom of pioneering thinkers like Warren Buffett, who famously counsels that "the stock market is a device for transferring money from the impatient to the patient." Silence, in this context, functions as a discipline—a deliberate choice to prioritise long-term vision over short-term noise, to accept uncertainty without panic, and to permit compounding to work its quiet magic.

One compelling real-world illustration is the rise of passive investing through index funds and robo-advisors. These tools embody silence by design: they eschew the noise of daily market speculation in favour of steady, algorithm-driven allocation aligned with strategic risk profiles. Their widespread adoption signals a growing recognition that *quiet consistency frequently outperforms frenetic engagement.* In addition, behavioural studies reveal that investors using automated, low-intervention platforms report less stress and greater satisfaction—corroborating that silence also benefits emotional well-being, a crucial yet often neglected dimension of financial health.

Yet, silence as a financial strategy requires overcoming cultural and psychological barriers. In a society that venerates hustle and rewards constant busyness, stillness can be misinterpreted as complacency or laziness. Financial media and social platforms amplify this bias by celebrating high-frequency trading stories and sensationalising market swings. Resisting this tide demands a recalibration of values: recognising that *true mastery involves discerning when to act and when to refrain.* This discernment cultivates what might be called "productive boredom"—the capacity to sit with uncertainty and allow the investment thesis to unfold without incessant interference.

Moreover, silence creates space for reflection and recalibration, essential elements of sound portfolio management. Periodic, deliberate review—rather than constant tinkering—enables investors to assess alignment with goals, risk tolerance, and life circumstances without being swayed by ephemeral market sentiments. This measured approach fosters resilience against volatility-induced anxiety and guards against the cognitive fatigue induced by relentless decision-making. It is here that silence transcends mere inactivity to become an active, thoughtful stance towards financial stewardship.

Critically, adopting silence does not mean disengagement from learning or strategic planning. Instead, it encourages *selective attention*—focusing on high-quality information and meaningful signals rather than the flood of data clamouring for immediate reaction. This shift echoes principles from disciplines such as mindfulness and systems thinking, where intentional attention to the present moment and overarching patterns yields better outcomes than fragmented, reactive responses. Investors who master this balance position themselves to navigate uncertainty with composure and insight.

This subchapter also explores the ethical and philosophical dimensions of silence in investing. By resisting the urge to constantly chase returns or micro-manage portfolios, investors affirm a commitment to stewardship that honours patience, humility, and long-term thinking. This mindset counters the predatory dynamics that characterise some aspects of contemporary finance and aligns investment practices with broader values of sustainability and social responsibility.

In sum, reclaiming silence as a financial strategy is both a practical imperative and a profound philosophical statement. It challenges the prevailing myth that constant action equates to competence and success. Instead, it champions *the power of quietude—the recognition that sometimes the best move is no move at all.* For the intelligent, time-conscious reader, this approach offers a pathway out of the exhausting cycle of over-engagement toward a more sustainable, effective, and humane form of investing.

Every paragraph here aims to deepen the reader's appreciation of silence not as absence but as presence—a cultivated space where patience, clarity, and trust enable wealth to grow organically. This is a call to rethink what it means to be active in finance, to value restraint as much as initiative, and to rediscover how *inaction, when chosen wisely, can become the new alpha.*

## What Gets Automated Gets Lived –

The notion that automation strips away humanity from our financial lives is a persistent misconception. Yet, in the evolving landscape of wealth management, *automation—far from erasing the human element—can deepen it by liberating us from the repetitive and distracting tasks that consume our attention.* When applied thoughtfully, systems-thinking enables individuals to reclaim time, mental energy, and emotional bandwidth, allowing for richer engagement with the aspects of life that truly matter. This subchapter unpacks how "what gets automated gets lived" is not merely a slogan but a powerful framework for enhancing both financial outcomes and personal fulfilment.

At the heart of this argument lies a fundamental reframing of automation's role. Rather than viewing automation as a cold, mechanical replacement for human judgement, it is more accurate to see it as a *partner in intentional living.* Automating routine financial processes—such as contributions, rebalancing, and tax optimisation—removes the cognitive load associated with constant decision-making. This reduction in mental friction translates into greater clarity and calm, enabling investors to focus on their broader goals and values. In other words, automation acts as a scaffolding that supports human intention rather than supplanting it.

Consider the psychological burden that comes from financial micromanagement. Daily monitoring, reacting to market noise, and recalibrating portfolios demand a level of vigilance that drains cognitive resources and induces stress. Research in behavioural finance shows that such decision fatigue often leads to suboptimal outcomes, including impulsive trades and emotional overreactions. By contrast, automation channels consistent, evidence-based strategies without the volatility of human emotion. The result is a quieter, more measured financial life that frees mental space for creative, strategic, and relational endeavours.

Real-world applications underscore this transformative potential. Robo-advisors like Betterment, Wealthfront, and Nutmeg exemplify systems-thinking in practice: they codify decades of academic research into algorithms that execute disciplined, low-cost, and tax-efficient investment strategies. Users of these platforms often report that the hands-off nature of their portfolios reduces anxiety and heightens their confidence in the financial plan. More importantly, they regain precious hours to devote to careers, family, and passions—areas where genuine human agency and meaning reside.

Beyond individual finance, systems-thinking and automation facilitate alignment between financial behaviour and life priorities. When routine financial operations are delegated to reliable mechanisms, individuals are more capable of engaging with questions of *why* they invest and *what* they hope to achieve beyond mere accumulation. This shift from process-oriented micromanagement to values-based reflection enhances the quality of decision-making, embedding money management within the broader context of life purpose.

Some critics argue that automation risks creating complacency or detachment, reducing investors to passive participants. Yet, this perspective overlooks the nuanced balance between *automation and active oversight.* Automation is not a substitute for engagement but a means to more intentional engagement. It liberates individuals from repetitive tasks, enabling them to monitor portfolio health, reassess goals, and adapt to life changes with greater presence and insight. Rather than diminishing humanity, it elevates it by clearing the path for deliberate choice and meaningful action.

Moreover, automation invites a systems-thinking mindset—a holistic perspective that recognises interdependencies, feedback loops, and long-term dynamics. This approach contrasts sharply with the fragmented, short-term focus often seen in manual investing. By automating rebalancing and contribution schedules, investors participate in a coherent system designed for resilience and compounding growth. This disciplined structure supports emotional stability by mitigating impulsive reactions to market volatility and reinforcing the primacy of consistent, incremental progress.

The enhancement of humanity through automation also resonates with contemporary theories in psychology and behavioural economics. Studies on cognitive load and decision fatigue reveal that when mundane decisions are externalised to systems, individuals experience reduced stress and improved well-being. This mental relief fosters better judgement in complex areas requiring creativity, empathy, and strategic thinking—qualities automation cannot replicate but certainly can nurture by removing distractions.

Importantly, automation's benefits extend beyond the individual to influence relationships and communities. Financial stress is a significant source of conflict within families and social networks. By embedding automated systems that ensure reliability and predictability, individuals can foster trust and reduce anxiety among dependents and partners. This structural stability allows interpersonal dynamics to flourish without the constant strain of financial uncertainty or micromanagement.

As automation permeates the financial domain, its ethical implications must also be considered. Systems-thinking encourages transparency, accountability, and inclusivity—principles essential to designing automation that respects user autonomy and promotes equitable access. Thoughtful automation empowers individuals to participate in financial markets with dignity and control, rather than surrendering agency to opaque algorithms or predatory practices.

In summary, the assertion that "what gets automated gets lived" captures a profound truth about the interplay between technology and humanity. By strategically automating repetitive and distracting financial tasks, investors can reclaim their cognitive and emotional resources, enabling richer, more authentic engagement with both their finances and their lives. Automation does not erase the human experience; it enhances it, offering a foundation upon which meaningful financial stewardship and personal flourishing can be built.

This perspective invites a recalibration of our relationship with technology in investing—not as a cold replacement for human insight but as a collaborative tool that clears the path for wisdom, creativity, and intentional living. It challenges readers to embrace systems-thinking not as a reduction of their role, but as an elevation of their capacity to live fully while managing wealth wisely.

## Your Life Beyond the Charts –

The pursuit of financial mastery often begins and ends with numbers—charts, graphs, performance metrics. Yet the most profound truth about investing is not found in these data points but beyond them, in the life that wealth is meant to support. *Your life beyond the charts is not merely a respite from managing money; it is the very reason for managing it at all.* This subchapter invites a vital reframing, encouraging readers to reclaim investing as a tool that serves human purpose rather than a purpose unto itself. In doing so, it offers reflections and practical prompts to reconnect financial strategy with the deeper dimensions of existence—meaning, relationships, creativity, and rest.

At first glance, the discipline of investing seems inherently numerical and abstract, demanding continual attention to market fluctuations and portfolio allocations. This focus on metrics and performance can easily narrow one's horizon to the point where financial outcomes eclipse broader life priorities. Yet, *wealth is fundamentally a means, not an end.* It functions as a form of leverage—creating freedom, security, and opportunity for experiences that define a life well lived. Recognising this distinction transforms the investor's role from a reactive tactician obsessed with short-term gains to a deliberate architect of a life enriched by, rather than enslaved to, financial goals.

The metaphor of "beyond the charts" underscores this shift. It suggests stepping back from the numbers' immediacy to observe the wider context they serve. This requires cultivating a mindset that embraces *financial silence and spaciousness*, allowing moments of stillness where purpose and values take centre stage. The wisdom literature of finance—from behavioural economics to stoic philosophy—reiterates the importance of such detachment. It cautions against over-identification with portfolio ups and downs, highlighting that emotional equilibrium and clarity often emerge only when one relinquishes the illusion of total control over markets.

One practical implication of this perspective is the embrace of systems that automate routine financial tasks, thereby liberating time and mental bandwidth. When the mechanics of investing—

contributions, rebalancing, tax optimisation—are entrusted to trustworthy frameworks, individuals are freed to focus on *questions that charts cannot answer*. What does a meaningful day look like? Which relationships merit investment of time and care? How might one nurture creative pursuits or contribute to community? These inquiries reaffirm that the ultimate purpose of managing wealth is to enhance human flourishing.

Consider real-world examples where investors who have internalised this philosophy demonstrate remarkable resilience and satisfaction. Research indicates that those who adopt value-driven approaches to wealth tend to exhibit lower stress and greater life satisfaction, even during market turbulence. They view financial setbacks not as existential threats but as temporary fluctuations within a broader narrative of purpose. Their portfolios become extensions of personal mission rather than mere accumulators of capital, and their relationship with money becomes one of service rather than servitude.

The chapter also challenges the pervasive cultural myth that financial success demands constant vigilance and active manipulation of markets. Instead, it posits *inaction as a strategic and psychologically sound posture*. This does not mean passivity or neglect but intentional patience—recognising that compounding, diversification, and disciplined saving, performed quietly and consistently, constitute the most effective route to enduring wealth. Such "silence" in investing parallels the silence needed for deep thinking, creativity, and authentic connection in life.

Critically, this reframing invites reflection on *what legacy means beyond financial bequests*. A richer life entails transmitting values, wisdom, and emotional habits alongside assets. How one relates to money in life—the humility, discipline, generosity, or anxiety demonstrated—forms an intangible inheritance that shapes the next generation's relationship with wealth. Investing thus becomes a practice not just of capital growth but of cultural and ethical transmission, demanding mindfulness and intentionality.

For readers seeking practical integration, this subchapter offers prompts to anchor financial decisions within personal narratives.

These include clarifying core values, articulating life aspirations beyond wealth, and designing rituals that connect money management with meaning. Such exercises counterbalance the often impersonal nature of investment metrics, grounding financial choices in the lived human experience.

Philosophically, the article aligns with contemporary thought emphasizing *the role of money as a servant to well-being rather than a master of existence*. It draws on cross-disciplinary insights from psychology, economics, and philosophy to illuminate how reconnecting with life's broader canvas fosters not only financial success but profound fulfilment. This approach transcends technical expertise, urging a holistic understanding of wealth as embedded in the complex fabric of human life.

Ultimately, "Your Life Beyond the Charts" reclaims the central truth that investing is not an endgame of figures and forecasts but a means to craft a life of purpose, presence, and peace. It invites readers to see beyond the tickers and trends to the quiet, essential realities that make financial strategy worthwhile—the moments of joy, connection, and rest that define the human condition. This perspective offers a vital corrective to the frenetic, numbers-driven narratives that dominate financial discourse, anchoring wealth in the profound richness of living itself.

# Conclusion
# Investing Is Not About Money

Investing is most often framed narrowly, as though its sole purpose were the relentless accumulation of wealth, a pursuit measured in percentages and currency. Yet beneath this conventional framing lies a deeper, almost philosophical question: what if investing is not truly about money at all? This chapter invites readers to shift focus from external markers of financial success to the inner landscape of lived experience. Here, the boundaries between finance and philosophy blur, prompting reflection not on balance sheets but on balance in life itself. What might it mean to place full trust in the systems you have created—rational, automated frameworks intended to steward your capital? What possibilities open when the preoccupation with funding recedes, allowing attention to return to the essential work of being human?

This move away from obsession with numerical gains is not a rejection of prudence or careful management. Rather, it is an appeal to a higher order of engagement. The ultimate purpose of investing lies not in amassing wealth but in creating conditions for a meaningful, well-lived life. Achieving this requires intellectual courage, challenging ingrained cultural assumptions that equate net worth with personal worth, or constant striving with success. Yet the payoff is profound: a liberation of presence, creativity, and relational depth, freed from the compulsion to micromanage every market fluctuation.

Trust is central to this perspective. To entrust your portfolio to thoughtfully designed systems is to recognise the limits of individual control—an act that is at once humble and wise. Such trust allows one to step back from incessant monitoring and reaction, freeing mental and emotional resources for pursuits beyond finance. This chapter explores how automation and intelligent system design function not as abdication but as partnership: a collaboration with reason, discipline, and data. Within this framework, life's subtleties—those aspects no algorithm can capture—become accessible.

The discussion weaves together insights from psychology, ethics, and behavioural economics to probe what it truly means to "live well" with wealth. It examines how attachment to money as an end can foster anxiety, disconnection, and distorted priorities. Conversely, it offers evidence and stories of individuals who have embraced financial systems as instruments of freedom and fulfilment, moving beyond the transactional toward something more transcendent.

Readers are invited to interrogate their own financial narratives: what stories do you tell yourself about money and identity? How might these narratives constrain or empower you? What would it mean to cultivate patience and acceptance alongside ambition? The text challenges the reader to move beyond performance chasing, instead fostering a sense of financial grace rooted in values, vision, and trust.

This perspective does not minimise the real complexities of managing wealth but situates them within a broader human context. Money shapes opportunities and imposes constraints, yet it must not overshadow the essential pursuits of health, connection, and meaning. The chapter offers a framework for integrating financial discipline with emotional intelligence and ethical reflection, advocating a holistic approach to money that honours both head and heart.

Ultimately, the invitation is to return to what one does best: being human. It is a call to reclaim agency—not over markets, but over time, attention, and relationships. Success, from this vantage, is measured not in returns or rankings but in the quality of lived experience that investing enables. This chapter functions both as a summation and a departure: grounding readers in enduring principles while pointing toward the ongoing work of designing a life that transcends spreadsheets and celebrates the richness of being.

Each paragraph is dense with insight, crafted to provoke reflection, clarify values, and inspire practical transformation. In its entirety, the chapter offers a guide to reimagining investing as a means to human flourishing—one that embraces paradox, tolerates uncertainty, and cultivates trust in systems, so readers may fully engage with the profound, ineffable richness of life beyond the charts.

**In this closing chapter, we leave the reader not with tools, but with questions:**

Trust is the fulcrum upon which the entire edifice of modern investing balances—a concept both deceptively simple and profoundly difficult. In this closing chapter, we confront the most essential questions that have quietly underpinned every insight offered thus far: *What would it mean to trust deeply in your system? What kind of life could you build if you ceased obsessing over its funding?* These questions invite us beyond the realm of technical mastery and financial acumen into a terrain where philosophy and finance intersect, where the measures of success transcend earnings to encompass the quality of living itself.

At the heart of this inquiry is the recognition that investment systems—whether robo-advisors, algorithmic models, or disciplined strategies—are designed to act with rationality, consistency, and an absence of human foibles. Yet the temptation to micromanage, to second-guess, or to surrender to anxiety remains persistent, often stemming from a fundamental mistrust not of the systems but of ourselves. To trust deeply is to release the grip of this mistrust, acknowledging that *our systems excel at what we cannot: unemotional decision-making rooted in data and time-tested principles.* Such trust does not mean passivity but rather the exercise of wisdom—knowing when to act and, crucially, when to step back.

Imagine the transformative potential of a life freed from the compulsive monitoring of every market twitch. Consider the cognitive and emotional bandwidth reclaimed when one relinquishes the illusion of omnipotent control over financial outcomes. This shift is not merely practical but existential. Investing ceases to be a relentless contest of wills against markets and becomes instead an enabling foundation for meaningful work, relationships, and rest. It is in this light that we understand investing not as a goal but as a tool—a means to create space for the pursuits that constitute a well-lived life.

This chapter explores how embracing trust in smart financial systems is an act of profound self-care and philosophical alignment. It challenges readers to interrogate their relationship with money and control: How much of your identity is tethered to your portfolio's fluctuations? What emotional costs are incurred by constant vigilance? By reflecting on these questions, readers can begin to disentangle their sense of self-worth from short-term financial performance.

Real-world examples underscore this transformation. Consider the experience of investors who weathered the 2008 financial crisis by adhering to their automated strategies, resisting the urge to panic-sell. Their willingness to trust their systems not only preserved capital but also afforded them the emotional composure to engage fully with life's demands beyond the market's volatility. Conversely, those who deviated in fear or hubris often suffered losses that echoed beyond their portfolios into personal well-being.

The chapter also delves into the ethical dimension of trust. Entrusting capital to a system implies responsibility—not only for one's own financial health but for the broader social and ecological contexts affected by investment choices. Modern intelligent systems increasingly incorporate Environmental, Social, and Governance (ESG) criteria, reflecting values that extend legacy beyond immediate returns. Thus, trust becomes an invitation to align financial action with deeper principles.

Further, the narrative examines the tension between technology and humanity. Far from displacing human agency, well-designed financial automation amplifies it by removing distraction and repetition, allowing individuals to focus on creativity, relationships, and self-reflection. This partnership reframes the investor's role from constant executor to thoughtful steward, balancing trust in systems with active engagement in life's richness.

Finally, the chapter offers reflective prompts, encouraging readers to articulate their own definitions of success and to envision lives where financial systems serve—not dominate—the human experience. It urges a pivot from anxiety-driven management to value-driven stewardship, from chasing returns to cultivating meaning.

This concluding exploration does not promise easy answers but invites an ongoing dialogue—between intellect and emotion, control and surrender, material security and existential freedom. It is an intellectual and emotional recalibration that equips readers not merely to manage portfolios but to design lives worthy of their fullest potential. The ultimate mastery lies not in commanding markets but in mastering the art of living well *through* them.

Every paragraph in this chapter is crafted to provoke thoughtful consideration, deepen insight, and inspire a reimagining of the relationship between finance and humanity. It stands as a capstone—a definitive guide to embracing investing as a facilitator of life, rather than its master.

# About the Author

Elias Hartwell writes at the intersection of money, meaning, and modern life. With a background in systems thinking and a lifelong fascination with how people relate to risk and time, Elias helps readers find emotional clarity in financial complexity. His work dismantles the illusion of control that permeates personal finance and invites a quieter, more deliberate relationship with wealth. When he's not writing, he's observing—markets, nature, behavior—always with a notebook in hand and a deep belief that simplicity isn't laziness; it's wisdom. Start Investing with Robo-Advisors is part of Elias's mission to humanize finance and give readers permission to let go of the noise and live with more intention.

www.ingramcontent.com/pod-product-compliance
Lightning Source LLC
Chambersburg PA
CBHW031349230926
51848CB00002B/444
*9789371771801*